Introduction to English Law

VisuaLaw Study Guide Volume 1

Markus McDowell
Jessica Patel

SULIS

Publications

This VisuaLaw Study Guide are based on the University of London Study Guide for Common Law Reasonings and Institutions (CLRI). This publication is an independent work, and is not connected with nor endorsed by the University.

Published by Sulis International
www.SulisInternational.com

INTRODUCTION TO ENGLISH LAW

ISBN-13: 978-0692680742
ISBN-10: 0692680748

First Edition: Apr 2016

1. Law   2. General

CONTENTS

PREFACE

Welcome to VisuaLaw Study Guide Volume 1: Introduction to English Law. This book contains three sections of material: Outlines, Diagrams, and Exam Study Sheets.

Research shows that to understand a subject well enough to take a law exam, mere repetition and memorization is not enough. A student must internalize the material and be able to recall details based on connections. These study guides are based on these principles.

Outlines are detailed outlines of the course material, arranged by topic, including statutes, cases, and key terms, arranged for aid in studying, memorizing, and revising/reviewing. Use these along with your textbook and other readings as you learn.

Diagrams are companions to the Course Outlines. These contain flow charts, diagrams, and other visual aids for each topic. Use these as a way to get the 'big picture' of each topic, and to test yourself by seeing if you can remember the details from the Outlines. Try redrawing the diagrams from memory.

Exam Study Sheets are condensed outlines, based on the Course Outlines. These can be used as another way of getting the big picture, but also for revising and testing yourself on the details. Each "sheet" contains 1–5 pages on each of the topics, including key statutes and cases.

These Study Guides are not intended as a substitute for required readings or any other assignments. Everything you need to know to pass the exams is not included here—this book is an outline of the subject and a companion study tool. If you understand and can discuss each element on each page, you will be well on your way to understanding the subject.

Send questions, errata, and suggestions to legalyankee@SulisInc.com. Your input will help us continue to update and refine these study guide.

COURSE OUTLINES

These Outlines present the topics and subtopics of the course in standard outline form, along with key terms, cases, and statutes.

Suggested study plan:

1. Look over the chapter which corresponds to the chapter you are about to study for your course.
2. Read your assigned readings and do any assigned activities. Peridically review the material in this Study Guide to reinforce the material.
3. Review the VisuaLaw Course Outline. Test yourself: are you able to discuss each item in detail? Go back over your reading material to strengthen the areas in which you are weak. Repeat until you have mastered the topic.
4. Repeat for each subject in the course.

When you are preparing for your exams, use the VisuaLaw Course Outlines to review the material you need to know, and guide you back to your course textbook and readings for information you need to review.

Markus McDowell & Jessica Patel

1. Introduction

1. What is Law?
    1.1. There are a lot of rules, norms, conventions, but only some of these are actually 'Law'
    1.2. the 'Law' concerned rules enforced by the State, not jus social conventions (though sometimes these overlap
        i. Not all laws are the same in every jurisdiction (i.e., adultery in England v in Iran
    1.3. The nature of law debate — philosophy of law

2. What is the Law's Purpose?
    2.1. Maintain order of society
    2.2. Partington: Macro-functions: public, optical social, economic, and moral order
    2.3. Partington: Micro functions: acceptable behavior (criminal and civil)
    2.4. Conflict of functions

3. Sources of Law
    3.1. Parliament
        i. Two chambers: House of Commons (elected) and House of Lords (appointed)
        ii. An Act of Parliament is a valid law = statute
        iii. Process: Green Paper - White Paper - debate/amendments and pass/fail - Royal Assent - Publication as an act
        iv. Takes precedent over common law or case law (not EU law)
        v. Primary legislation = acts of Parliament or Statutes
        vi. Secondary legislation = detailed rules under an Act: statutory instrument (regulations, rules, orders)
    3.2. Courts
        i. common law = the law as decided by judges
        ii. In contrast to statute law passed by Parliament
        iii. Established by judges in individual cases
        iv. Developed over many years, to origins of English common law in the 12th century

v. "The Common Law is to be found in the records of our several courts of justice in books of reports and judicial decisions, and in treatises of learned sages of the profession, prescribed and handed down to us from the times of ancient antiquity. They are the laws which gave rise and origin to that collection of maxims and customs which is now known by the name of common law." (Sir William Blackstone 1723–1780, *Commentaries on the laws of England*)

vi. Common law is a system used in many countries (e.g., England, Wales, USA, Candid, Australia); different from "Civil Law" used other countries (France, Germany, Italy). (Do not confuse "Civil Law" as a description of an entire legal system, with 'civil law' (along with 'criminal law') in a common law system.)

3.3. EU

i. An economic and political agreement between 28 European countries, based on treaties between them all.

ii. has the rule of law as its basis

iii. All members of the EU are required to keep the laws of the EU (UK joined in 1973)

    a. Laws are enacted by the European Parliament, European Council and European Commission

    b. in the case of conflicts of law with a State's laws, EU law prevails

    c. Supremacy of EU law case

      - *R v Secretary of State for Transport, ex p Factortame (No 2)* [1991] 1 All ER 70, HL/ ECJ and *R v Secretary of State for Transport, ex p Factortame (No 3)* [1991] 3 All ER 769, ECJ

      - Merchant Shipping Act 1988 was ruled as contrary to EU law

      - See also *R v Secretary of State for Employment, ex p Equal Opportunities Commission* [1995] 1 AC 1

3.4. The European Convention on Human Rights (ECHR)

i. An international treaty signed in 1953 by members of the Council of Europe (separate from the EU)

ii. 47 countries have signed it (including UK in 1953)

iii. Human Rights Act 1998 incorporated the main provisions of the ECHR into domestic law

    a. Right to life (Art 2)

    b. Prohibition of Torture (Art 4)

    c. Prohibition of slavery and forced labour (art 5)

    d. Right to liberty and security (Art 5)

    e. Right to a fair trial (Art 6)

    f. No punishment without law (Art 7)

    g. Right to respect of family and private life (Art 8)

    h. Freedom of thought, conscience, and religion (Art 9)

    i. Freedom of expression (Art 10)

    j. Freedom of assembly and association (Art 11)

    k. Prohibition of discrimination (Art 14)

    l. Right not to be subjected to the death penalty (Arts 1, 2 of Protocol 6)

    m. Right to free elections (Art 3 of Protocol 1)

iv. Derogation

    a. Some of these rights are absolute and inalienable —they cannot be interfered with by a State

      - Arts 2, 3, 4, 7, 14

    b. Some are contingent — a state can derogate (opt out in some situations)

v. 'Margin of Appreciation'

    a. To help work out problems with the law because of the diverse cultural and legal traditions of the States

    b. Give States a degree of discretion, oversee by the European Court of Human Rights

    c. Examples

      - *Lautsi v Italy* (Application no. 30814/06) — presence of crucifixes in Italian schoolrooms does not violate Art 9

vi. Proportionality

    a. The EU's interference in the application of derogable provisions must be necessary and not go beyond what is absolutely necessary.

    b. "... every intrusion by the State upon the freedom of the individual stands in need of justification. Accordingly, any interference which is greater than required for the State's proper purpose cannot be justified. This is at the core of proportionality; it articulates the discipline which proportionality imposes on decision makers." (Lord Justice Laws at Hamlyn Lectures in 2013)

    c. *de Freitas v Permanent Secretary of Ministry of Agriculture, Fisheries, Lands and Housing* [1999] 1 AC 69

- the legislative objective is sufficiently important to justify limiting a fundamental right
- the measures designed to meet the legislative objective are rationally connected to it, and
- iii. the means used to impair the right or freedom are no more than is necessary to accomplish the objective.

4. Types of Legal Systems
4.1. Legal Traditions
    i. Religious; common law; civil/Roman law; socialist law
4.2. Civil Law (Continental) Systems
    i. Oldest type of law in history
    ii. Origins in Roman law
    iii. Codified system of law(EG civil code, codes covering corporate law, administrative law, tax law,)
    iv. Written constitutions based on specific codes
    v. Only legislative enactments are considered binding for all
    vi. There is little scope for judge made law, although judges generally follow precedent
    vii. Constitutional courts that can nullify laws and decisions of which are binding
4.3. Common Law Systems
    i. Introduction
        a. Roots in 11th century England
        b. Decisions of courts in individual cases make up binding law over time
        c. Documented in yearbook and law reports
        d. Key features of common law systems
          - Not always a written constitution or codified laws
          - Judicial decisions are binding, High court decisions can only be overturned by itself, or through legislation
          - If something is not expressly prohibited by law, It is permitted
    ii. History of Common Law
        a. Before the Norman conquest in 1066, law consisted of oral customs which vary from region to region
        b. Each shire had its own local court and follow local customs
        c. The Norman conquest brought the creation of the Kings court (*Curia Regis*)
          - Consisted of the King and advisers and landowners

and clerics
- Traveled around the country to hear grievances
d. Henry II in 1154 created a single system of justice for the country
    - Kept five judges in Westminster
    - Send the rest out around the country, Applying the law that was decided by judges and Westminster (the common law)
e. Eventually the laws began to be written down, the practice of using precedents began to be used in courts

> Common law courts grew up gradually as offshoots of the authority of the King and, as the very word 'court' indicates, these courts of justice were originally a part of the Royal Court. They were not created by law in order to administer pre-existing laws. They were created, or grew up, in order to solve pressing practical questions – to dispose of arguments, to solve disputes, and to suppress violence and theft. As they developed into what we would today recognize as courts of law, they actually created the law as they went along. Eventually their decisions began to fall into regular and predictable patterns, people began to take notes of what the judges were deciding, and in due course there emerged the modern 'law reports'. (P.S. Atiyah, Law and modern society. (Oxford: Oxford University Press, 1995))

c. Common law's contributions to social order
    a. The courts began to do away with the vendetta and feud system of establishing justice
    b. The courts punished criminals, and gave a peaceful means of land and property disputes
    c. Addressing these problems through the courts rather than through violence brought stability to the state
d. Equity
    a. The word equity means fair or just, In law it is particular set of legal rules used in courts
    b. By the 15th century, the Chancellor (a cleric) is the one who heard cases instead of the King
    c. A court of Chancery was set up to deal with petitions to the king
    d. The standard for the Chancellor what's what was morally right, not based on any precedent in prior cases
    e. The first decree in the chancellor's name was issued in 1474, and began the Court of Chancery operating under

rules of equity, Which were different than the common-law

- Equity created new rights (trust, beneficiaries, trustees, etc.)
- Equity created new remedies (compensation, damages, specific performance, injunction) based on the idea of putting right a wrong that had been done to someone

f. By the 19th century the Court of Chancery had become expensive and cases were lengthy

> *'This is the Court of Chancery, which has its decaying houses and its blighted lands in every shire, which has its worn-out lunatic in every madhouse and its dead in every churchyard, which has its ruined suitor with his slipshod heels and threadbare dress borrowing and begging through the round of every man's acquaintance, which gives to monied might the means abundantly of wearying out the right, which so exhausts finances, patience, courage, hope, so overthrows the brain and breaks the heart, that there is not an honourable man among its practitioners who would not give – who does not often give – the warning, 'Suffer any wrong that can be done you rather than come here!'* (Extract from Chapter 1 of* Bleak House *by Charles Dickens)*

g. In 1873, the courts of equity were combined with the common law courts (Judicature Act 1873-1875)

- All courts deal with the common law and equitable principles and remedies
- There is still a court of Chancery which deals with issues that rely heavily on equity (company law, conveyancing, property, wills and probate).

5. Legal Classification

5.1. Meaning of the term 'Common Law'

i. In contrast to Statute Law — the law found in decisions of courts rather than acts of Parliament

ii. In contrast to Equity — despite the two distinct bodies being combined, equitable principles and remedies are still different from common law principles and remedies

iii. In contrast to Civil Law — the differences between English common law legal systems and civil law Systems derived from Roman law.

5.2. Public law and private law

i. Public law deals with the relationship between citizens and their state
   a. Judicial review is the process where citizens can challenge decisions of the state
   b. Example: *R v Lord Chancellor ex p Witham* [1997] 2 All ER 779 where a court held that the Lord Chancellor acted Beyond his powers buy negating a provision that low income people were exempt from paying court fees
ii. Private law addresses relationships between individuals in which the state is not directly involved (contrasts, law land, probate, etc)

5.3. Criminal law and civil law
   i. Inside most common law Systems are to other systems referred to as criminal law in civil law
      a. Criminal law
         - part of public law where the state brings an individual before the court for actions considered against society
         - The state prosecutes in the name of the king or queen
         - The standard of proof required for a case to be proved is beyond a reasonable doubt
      b. Civil law
         - Part of private law where citizens or businesses resolve their disputes before a court
         - The standard of proof required is on the balance of probabilities
         - Civil law can be divided into contract law (agreements between parties), law of tort (damage caused by one party against another), Family law (disagreements involving domestic relationships between people), land law (property law, ownership of land or thing on it)

6. Constitution and the Legal System
6.1. The constitution
   i. A constitution refers to the way in which a country's laws in courts are organized and proceed
   ii. Some are written and some are not. Somewhere in one document, Some are spread out among the documents, or even are based on conventions
   iii. The US and Germany have written constitutions in a single document

iv. The UK has rules and principles spread over a number of written materials, statutes, common law, customs, and constitutional conventions

6.2. Principles

i. Separation of powers — the three powers or branches of a system should be separate and form checks and balances between them

    a. The legislature makes new laws (Statutes)

    b. The executive implements the law and runs the country

    c. The judiciary hears legal disputes and interprets legislation

    d. *'When the legislative and executive powers are united in the same person, or in the same body of magistrates, there can be no liberty ... there is no liberty if the powers of judging is not separated from the legislative and executive ... there would be an end to everything, if the same man or the same body ... were to exercise those three powers.'* (Montesquieu, *The Spirit of Laws* (c.1748))

    e. The Constitutional Reform Act 2005 strengthened the separation of powers by creating a separate Supreme Court and replacing the Lord Chancellor with a lord Chief Justice as head of the judiciary in England and Wales, Among other things

ii. Judicial independence

    a. Judges decide cases without interference from the executive or legislative

    b. The judiciary should be accountable

    c. The judiciary should be independent

    d. "The citizen must be able to challenge the legitimacy of executive action before an independent judiciary. Because it is the executive that exercises the power of the State and because it is the executive, in one form or another, that is the most frequent litigator in the courts, it is from executive pressure or influence that the judiciary are particularly to be protected." Lord Phillips, first President of the UK Supreme Court (2011).

    e. s3 CRA 2005: "The Lord Chancellor, other ministers of the Crown, and all with responsibility for matters relating to the judiciary or otherwise to the administration of justice must uphold the continued independence of the judiciary."

iii. Parliamentary Sovereignty
  a. Course cannot overrule legislation
  b. Parliament passes laws that feature parliament cannot change
  c. (however EU law has priority over national laws that pertain to it)
  d. Parliamentary statutes take precedence over common-law
  e. Where there is a conflict between statute and common law, statute Will prevail

iv. The Rule of Law
  a. The constitutional concept that a citizen can only be punished if proved in court they violated the law
  b. No person is above the law
  c. Lord Bingham's eight ingredients of the rule of law
    - It must be accessible, intelligible, clear and predictable
    - Questions of legal rights and liability should normally be resolved by the application of law rather than the exercise of discretion
    - The laws of the land should apply equally to all, except where objective differences justify differentiation
    - The law must give adequate protection to human rights
    - Some means should be provided for the resolution of civil disputes that do not involve excessive cost or delay
    - Ministers and public officers must exercise their powers reasonably, in good faith, for the purpose for which the powers were conferred and without exceeding the limits of such powers
    - The adjudicative procedures provided by the state should be fair
    - The state must comply with its obligations in international law
  d. Judicial independence and the rule of law
    - Bangalore Principles of Judicial Conduct (adopted in 2002):
      • "Judicial independence is a prerequisite to the rule of law and a fundamental guarantee of a fair trial. A judge shall therefore uphold and exemplify judicial independence in both its individual and

institutional aspects."
- Individual and institutional independence (the state of mind of the judge, the relationship between the Judiciary and other branches)

e. The importance of the rule of law
- "... it is the underlying framework of rules and rights that make prosperous and fair societies possible. The rule of law is a system in which no one, including government, is above the law; where laws protect fundamental rights; and where justice is accessible to all ... Where the rule of law is weak, medicines fail to reach health facilities, criminal violence goes unchecked, laws are applied unequally across societies, and foreign investments are held back. Effective rule of law helps reduce corruption, improve public health, enhance education, alleviate poverty, and protect people from injustices and dangers large and small. Strengthening the rule of law is a major goal of governments, donors, businesses, and civil society organizations around the world." (World Justice Project, Introduction to Rule of Law Index 2014)
- Four universal principles
  • The government and its officials and agents as well as individuals and private entities are accountable under the law.
  • The laws are clear, publicized, stable, and just; are applied evenly; and protect fundamental rights, including the security of persons and property.
  • The process by which the laws are enacted, administered, and enforced is accessible, fair, and efficient.
  • Justice is delivered timely by competent, ethical, and independent representatives and neutrals who are of sufficient number, have adequate resources, and reflect the makeup of the communities they serve.
- Factors that should be evident:
  • Limited government powers
  • Absence of corruption
  • Order and security

- Fundamental rights
- Open government
- Civil justice
- Criminal justice

7. Justice

7.1. Fair justice and fair process

   i. Procedural fairness

   ii. Fairness in decision-making

   iii. The laws should be known and the accused have an opportunity to defend themselves

   iv. Law and facts

      a. It is the courts job to determine the facts of the case and apply the relevant law

      b. "questions of fact" are those which attempt to prove what happened

      c. "questions of law" are those which refer to legal principles but maybe argued in the case and the procedural rules for how it will be handled

   v. Substantive and procedural law

      a. Substantive law is that which defines, regulates, and creates the rights and obligations of people

      b. Procedural law is that which defines the steps to be taken, and how they are to be taken, throughout the judicial process of any given case.

7.2. Inquisitorial and adversarial procedure

   i. Common law court procedures, As opposed to civil law court procedures, are adversarial

      a. Each party is responsible for preparing their case and presenting it in court

      b. The role of the judge is to ensure procedures are followed and giving decision at the end based on the legal merits

   ii. Civil law jurisdictions engage in a more inquisitorial procedure

      a. The judge decides on witnesses and is responsible for investigating the facts

      b. Judges may examine witnesses and the litigants have no right of cross-examination.

2. The Courts

1. Distinctions
    1.1. Criminal and Civil Courts
        i. Civil courts resolve disputes between private citizens or between the citizen and the state
            a. E.g., breach of contract, injury claims, property rights, disputes about public authority actions
            b. The claimant is the person bringing the claim
            c. The defendant is the person defending the claim
        ii. Criminal courts determine cases where people are accused of breaking criminal laws
            a. The prosecution brings the case on behalf of of the state
            b. The defendant is the person defending against the state
            c. The court can fine or imprisonment the defendant if found guilty
            d. Most prosecutions are brought by the Crown Prosecution Service, but there are other state agencies
    1.2. Courts of First Instance and Appellate Courts
        i. Appeal court (appellate court): Once a decision is made, it be appealed to a higher court (civil and criminal)
        ii. First instance is the court which first heard and ruled on the case
    1.3. Judgments
        i. In some courts, judges sit in panels of three, five, seven, or nine
        ii. A Unanimous judgment is one in which all judges agreed on the decision
        iii. A dissenting judgment is one in which one (or more) judges disagree
        iv. A concurrent judgment is wanting which a judge agrees with the decision, but for slightly different reasons

2. Hierarchy
    2.1. The United Kingdom Supreme Court (established by the Constitutional Reform Act 2005 Part 3, came into being in October 2009)
        i. Replaced the House of Lords Appellate Committee (usually just 'House of Lords'

    ii. Highest court of appeal in the UK (except criminal cases from Scotland)

    iii. President is head of the Court

    iv. Called upon at times to rule on EU law

    v. Supposed to apply the EU laws that are relevant

    vi. Can ask EU courts for opinions and help

    vii. Party an appeal to ECHR after UKSC appeal is lost

2.2. Judicial Committee of the Privy Council

    i. The highest court of appeal for most Commonwealth countries, UK overseas territories, Crown dependencies, and military base areas

    ii. It applies the laws of the country or territory where the appeal originated

    iii. The judges are from the Supreme Court and sometimes with judges from constituent jurisdictions

2.3. Courts of Appeal

    i. Court of Appeal Civil Division

        a. Master of the role's is the head of the court

        b. The judges are known as Lord or Lady Justice of Appeal

        c. Mostly deal with appeals from first instance cases in the High Court and County courts

    ii. Court of Appeal Criminal Division

        a. Lord chief justice is the head of this division

        b. The judges are known as the Lords justices of appeal

        c. The court hears appeals against conviction or sentence from the Crown Court, And issues guidances for the lower courts

2.4. High Courts (hears criminal and civil cases at first instance and on appeal)

    i. Queen's Bench

        a. The the Largest of the three divisions

        b. Presiding over by the Lord chief justice

        c. 70 judges called High Court judges or *puisne* judges

        d. Hears cases in tort, contract, admiralty, commercial disputes, Technology and construction disputes, and includes an administrative court for judicial review

    ii. Chancery

        a. The Chancellor of the High Court leads this division

        b. There are 18 *puisne* judges

        c. Hear cases concerning bankruptcy, ownership of land, trusts and just speeded wills, patents

  iii. Family
    a. The President is the head of this division
    b. Includes 19 *puisne* judges
    c. Hear cases involving matrimony, adoption and other children's issues

2.5. Crown Court
  i. Both appellate and first instance
  ii. About 70 locations around England
  iii. Mostly serious criminal offenses
  iv. Appeals from magistrates Court
  v. Includes judges from the High Court, Circuit judges, and recorders (part-time circuit judges)
  vi. Criminal cases usually have a jury

2.6. Family Court
  i. Established by the Crime and Courts Act 2013 and The Family Procedure (Amendment No) Rules 2013/3204
  ii. Deals with family cases that previously would have been heard by the High Court, County courts, and magistrate court
  iii. The judges come from the High Court, and circuit judges, recorders, district judges, and magistrates

2.7. County Courts
  i. About 200 in England and Wales
  ii. Circuit judges, recorders, and district judges
  iii. Deal only with civil law: contract, tort, insolvency, probate, etc.

2.8. Magistrate Courts
  i. Professional District Judges, Magistrate court (assisted by professionally qualified clerk)
  ii. Unpaid, part time lay judges
  iii. Almost all criminal cases (preliminary before being sent to High Court), range of civil cases

2.9. Tribunals
  i. Particular grievances or specialist matters
  ii. Does not administer any part of the judicial power of the state (A-G v British Broadcasting Corporation, 3 All ER 61 (1980).
  iii. Specialist bodies dealing with specialist law
  iv. Led by chairman, usually a lawyer with two other members who represent the interest groups familiar with issue
  v. objectives and distinct characteristics (variety)
  vi. Other - ADR

2.10. Coroners

    i. Lawyers or medical practitioners
    ii. May have a jury of 7 or 11
    iii. Matters of sudden deaths
    iv. Inquisitorial process

3. European Courts

  3.1. Court of Justice of the European Union (CJEU
    i. This court is superior to the UK Supreme Court in disputes about European law
    ii. Established in 1954
    iii. One judge from each member state and eight advocates general
    iv. Since in Luxembourg
    v. Hears cases about breaches of obligations under European treaties, interpretation of European law

  3.2. European Court of Human Rights (ECtHR)
    i. Hears cases about breaches of the ECHR
    ii. Based in Strasbourg
    iii. Judges are elected by the Council of Europe for six year terms
    iv. The first stage of a case determines whether a case should be admitted to the full-court (3 judge panel)
    v. The second stage consists of seven judges who rule on the case (sometimes I 17 judge Grand Chamber hears the case)
    vi. This court has no authority over the English courts, but the HRA 1998 means that the court's decisions are taken into consideration (the Supreme Court usually follows the decisions of this court)
      a. Example: *Chester* [2013] UKSC 63.

3. Precedent

1. Introduction
    1.1. Doctrine of Judicial Precedent
      i. Binding precedent
      ii. stare decisis
      iii. Binding and persuasive precedent
        a. *Ratio* of the Privy Council
        b. *Ratio* of superior courts in other jurisdictions of the common-law
        c. High court judges referring to decisions by other High Court judges
      iv. Vertical and horizontal
        a. Vertical precedent
        b. Horizontal precedent
      v. *ratio decidendi* and *obiter dicta*
    1.2. Material facts
    1.3. Distinguishing
    1.4. Loss of binding authority
    1.5. Identifying the *ratio decidendi*

2. The courts and precedent
    2.1. The Judge-Made Doctrine
    2.2. Do Judges Make Law or Declare What It Is?
      i. William Blackstone
      ii. *Midland Silicone Ltd v Scruttons Ltd* [1962] AC 446.
      iii. Lord Reid, *The Judge as Law Maker*
      iv. *National Westminster Bank v Spectrum Plus* [2005] 2 AC 680

3. In practice
    3.1. Vertical and Horizontal Precedent
      i. Vertical
      ii. Horizontal
        a. Until 1898 the House of Lords (now UKSC) held it was not bound by its own decisions
        b. *London Street Tramways Ltd v London County Council* [1898] AC 375
      iii. The Practice Statement (Judicial Precedent) [1966] 3 All ER

77

iv. Horizontal in the UKSC
  a. *Austin v Southwark London Borough Council* [2010] UKSC 28, [2010] 4 All ER 16
v. Caution since the Practice Statement
vi. Examples
  a. *Knuller v DPP* [1973] AC 435
  b. *R v Shivpuri* [1986] 2 All ER 334
  c. *British Railways Board v Herrington* [1972] AC 877
  d. *Murphy v Brentwood District Council* [1990] 2 All ER 908; *Anns v Merton London Borough* [1977] 2 All ER 492.
  e. *Austin v Mayor and Burgesses of the London Borough of Southwark* [2010] UKSC 28 and s.82(2) of the Housing Act 1985
3.2. Vertical in the CoA (Civil Division)
  i. Lord Denning's arguments
  ii. *Cassell & Co Ltd v Broome* [1972] AC 1027
3.3. Horizontal in the CoA (Civil Division)
  i. Bound by its previous decisions, with some exceptions as described in *Young v Bristol Aeroplane Co Ltd* [1944] 2 All ER 293
    a. Conflicting decisions: *National Westminster Bank v Powney* [1990] 2 All ER 416; *Tiverton Estates Ltd v Wearwell Ltd* [1974] 1 All ER 209.
    b. Conflicting with later HoL/UKSC decision
      - implied overruling
    c. *per incuriam* decisions
      - *Morelle v Wakeling* [1955] 2 QB 379, 406
  ii. Court of Appeal decision is in conflict with it earlier decision of the Supreme Court.
    a. *Miliangos v George Frank (Textiles) Ltd* [1976] AC 443 and *Schorsch Meier GmbH v Hennin* [1975] QB 416 and *Havanah*, 1960.
  iii. Should CoA be able to depart from its own earlier decision?
    a. *Gallie v Lee* [1969] 1 All ER 1062
    b. Settled in *Davis v Johnson* [1978] 1 All ER 841 (CA), [1978] 1 All ER 1132 (HL).
3.4. Horizontal in the CoA (Criminal Division)
  i. *R v Taylor* [1950] 2 All ER 170; *Young v Bristol Aeroplane*
3.5. Divisional Courts of the High Court

    i. Vertical - divisional courts of the High Court are bound by House of Lords, Supreme Court, Court of Appeal; decisions of the divisional courts are binding on courts below it

    ii. Horizontal - divisional courts are bound by their own decisions, but *Young v Bristol Aeroplane* can be applied

    iii. High Court - bound by the House of Lords, Supreme Court, court of Appeal, divisional courts. The high courts own decisions are highly persuasive, but not bound by them

    iv. Crown Court - bound by all courts above it, By its own decisions, and binds all courts below it

    v. Privy Council

        a. Privy Council decisions do not bind other courts, but are persuasive

        b. But see *R v James and Karimi* [2006] EWCA Crim 14; *R v Smith (Morgan James)* [2001] 1 AC 146; *AG for Jersey v Holley* [2005] UKPC 23

4. The ECHR and the UKSC

    4.1. Introdoction

        i. s. 2(1) HRA 1998: UK court must "take into account"

            a. *R (on the application of Alconbury Developments Ltd v Secretary of State for the Environment, Transport and the Regions* [2001] UKHL 23

            b. *R v Horncastle* [2009] UKSC 14

    4.2. Changes to the HRA 1998?

        i. Oct 2014 - proposals for reform -

        ii. Dec 2014 - results of opting out of ECHR

        iii. May 2015 - PM Cameron announced intention to repeal the HRA 1998 and replaced with a British Bill of Rights.

5. Judges as law-makers

    5.1. UKSC takes a cautious approach

    5.2. 'democratic deficit.'

    5.3. Examples of judicial decisions both in overruling and in caution

        i. *R v R (Marital Exemption)* [1992] 1 AC 599; *R v Brown* [1993] 2 All ER 75; *Nicklinson and Lamb v Ministry of Justice* [2013] EWCA Civ 961

6. The history of law-making

    6.1. Year Books

    6.2. Private Reports

6.3. Law Reports

7. Writing a Case Note

7.1. ID the case (citation)

7.2. Court

7.3. date

7.4. Names

   i. Parties

   ii. Judges

   iii. Optional: solicitors/barristers acting for parties

7.5. Material facts

7.6. Procedural history

7.7. Every judgment or opinion

   i. Decision reached by each judge

   ii. Reason for decision

   iii. Majority, minority, Leading, dissenting

7.8. Summary of majority decision

7.9. Summary of dissenting opinion

7.10. Whether strong case in doctrine of precedent

4. Statutory Interpretation

1. Introduction

1.1. An important part of the judiciary's function is to interpret statutes passed by Parliament

1.2. Statutory interpretation guidelines have been built over the years

    i. e.g., In *Sussex Peerage Claim* (1844), Tindal CJ wrote:

    ii. "The only rule for the construction of Acts of Parliament is that they should be construed according to the intent of the Parliament which passed the Act."

1.3. Two difficulties in this process

    i. Meanings of words are not always clear or unambiguous; can have a number of different meanings; change over time

    ii. It is not always clear what Parliament's intention was in passing a law

2. The Difficulty

2.1. Bennion, *Staute Law*, listed four features of statutes that make interpretation difficult

    i. Ellipsis - the writers left out certain words because they thought they were implied

    ii. Broad terms

    iii. Unforeseeable developments due to social or economic changes

    iv. Errors in printing or drafting

3. Reasons for Interpretation

3.1. A Judge's interpretation can make a difference in how the law is applied

3.2. Judge must determine the meaning, scope, and applicability of a statute to a given context

3.3. Dicey wrote, "Statutes themselves, though manifestly the work of Parliament, often receive more than half their meaning from judicial decisions. (*Lectures on the relation between law and public opinion in England during the nineteenth century*. (1905, 2001), 486)

4. Approaches

4.1. Literal Rule (Literalism)

i. Apply the ordinary meaning of words

ii. Lord Esher MR, *R v The Judge of the City of London Court* [1892] 1 QB 273 - "If the words of an Act are clear, you must follow them, even though they lead to a manifest absurdity. The court has nothing to do with the question whether the legislature has committed an absurdity."

iii. Ancient example: *R v Harris* (1836) 7 Car & P 446, 173 ER 198 where the defendant has bit off the victim's nose had not violated the offense which read "unlawfully and maliciously stab, cut or wound any person" — an instrument had to be used to have violated the statute.

iv. Modern example: *R v Maginnis* [1987] 1 All ER 907 (HL) interpreting s.5(3) Misuse of Drugs Act 1971: "It is an offence for a person to have a controlled drug in his possession, whether lawfully or not, with intent to supply it to another ..."

    a. cannibis resin was found in defendant's car, which he said did not below to him, left by friend.

    b. Court (on appeal) held that, literally, a person who is left with drugs and intends to return them is 'supplying" them.

    c. Dissenting judgment: "... I do not feel able to say that either the delivery of goods by a depositor to a depositee, or the redelivery of goods by a depositee to a depositor, can sensibly be described as an act of supplying goods to another. I certainly cannot conceive of myself using the word 'supply' in this context in ordinary speech. In ordinary language the cloakroom attendant, the left luggage officer, the warehouseman and the shoe mender do not 'supply' to their customers the articles which those customers have left with them."

v. Example: *R v Brown* [1996] 1 All ER 545 (HL) interpreting s.5(2)(b) of the Data Protection Act 1984: "it is an offence knowingly or recklessly to use personal data other than for the purpose described in the relevant entry in the register of data users..."

    a. police officer used a national computer to check registrations of people who owed a friend's debt collection company, but no evidence he passed he info to the friend.

    b. Majority of judges held that he had not 'used' the

information, only accessed it (literal approach)

    c. Dissenting minority: the word 'use' should be given broader meaning because the purpose of the Act was protection of privacy (this is called a purposed approach, see below)

4.2. Golden Rule

    i. Uses the literary approach, but if this results in an 'absurd' result, the words can be modified

    ii. Lord Wensleydale, *Grey v Pearson* (1857) 6 HL Cas 106: "... the grammatical and ordinary sense of words is to be adhered to, unless that would lead to some absurdity, or some repugnance or inconsistency with the rest of the instrument, in which case the grammatical and ordinary sense of the words may be modified so as to avoid the absurdity and inconsistency, but no further."

    iii. Example: *Adler v George* [1964] 2 QB 7 interpreting s.3 of the Official Secrets Act 1920, where it was an offense to obstruct the Queen's forces in the vicinity of a prohibited place. Defendant argued that he was *in* an offense place, not in the *vicinity* of it. Court held that the word 'vicinity' had to be also 'in' the place, otherwise the law is absurd.

    iv. See also *Re Sigsworth* [1935] Ch 89.

4.3. Mischief Rule

    i. The most ancient approach, described in *Heydon's Case* (1584) 3 Co Rep 7a, 76 ER 637

    ii. First, review the state of the common law before the Act was passed

    iii. Second, determine the wrongdoing the Act was intended to address

    iv. Third, interpret the law in light of that intended purpose (this is similar to the purpose rule below)

    v. Example: *Smith v Hughes* [1960] 2 All ER 859, interpreting s.1 Street Offences Act 1959, 'It shall be an offence for a common prostitute to loiter or solicit in a street or public place for the purposes of prostitution.'

        a. Defendant was inside a house, tapping on a window to attract passerby, therefore, she was not soliciting 'in the street'

        b. Lord Parker CJ wrote, 'For my part I approach the matter by considering what is the mischief aimed at by this Act. Everybody knows that it was an Act intended to clean up the streets, to enable people to walk along the streets without being molested by common prostitutes.'

4.4. Purposive

  i. Takes a wider view by deciding what Parliament intended to achieve by writing and passing the law—'the spirit of the Act'

  ii. Denning LJ, *Magor & St Mellons RDC v Newport Corporation* [1950] 2 All ER 1226 (CA); [1952] AC 189 (HL), 'We do not sit here to pull the language of Parliament to pieces and to make nonsense of it. That is an easy thing to do and a thing to which lawyers are too often prone. We sit here to find out the intention of Parliament and of ministers and carry it out, and we do this better by filling in the gaps and making sense of the enactment than by opening it up to destructive analysis.'

  iii. Criticism of this approach is that it can give judges freedom to deviate from the language of an Act (in the HoL appeal, Lord Simonds wrote that this approach is a 'naked usurpation of the legislative function.'

  iv. This approach has gained more ground, perhaps because of the requirements of having to rely on EU legislation.

  v. In addition, the case of *Pepper v Hart* [1993] 1 All ER 42 allowed that courts could rely on legislative material outside of the Act itself to determine the intent of Parliament (such as Hansard)

    a. See also *R (on the application of Quintavalle) v Secretary of State for Health* [2003] 2 AC 687

4.5. Giving Effect to the Intention of Parliament

  i. This is the constitutional role of the judiciary

  ii. Judges have different views as to how to approach that task

5. Aids

5.1. Presumptions

  i. Examples

    a. Statutes are not retrospective (esp in criminal law) —one cannot be accused of an illegal act that occurred before Parliament made it illegal.

      - Exception: s.58(8) of the Criminal Justice Act 2003 - allows prosecution to appeal against acquittal

    b. Changes to basic rules must be clearly defined

      - If a change to the common law is not made clear by an Act of Parliament, the common law principle applies

- See *Leach v R* [1912] AC 305

5.2. Language
  i. *Ejusdem generis*
      a. general words that follow specific words should be read in light of the preceding specific words
      b. Example: Sunday Observance Act 1677 - 'no tradesman, artificer, workman, labourer **or other person whatsoever**, [shall work on Sundays]'
      c. If the law meant that no one was to work on Sundays, then it would have been easier just to say that. This, the first four words define the latter, which mean the general word refer to others in that same class of workers
  ii. Noscitur a socciis
      a. Words should be given the meaning that derives from the immediate context
      b. Example: *Pengelly v Bell Punch Co Ltd* [1964] 2 All ER 945 interpreting s.28 of the Factories Act 1961
          - The Act stated "Floors, steps, stairs passageways and gangways [must be kept free from obstruction].'
          - Court held that this did not mean to include areas which were meant for storage of items

5.3. Internal texts
  i. Anything in an Act may be used to interpret it: long title, short title, preamble, etc.
  ii. Can help understand purpose of act

5.4. External sources
  i. Hansard Reports
      a. Since 1992, courts may consult the reports of debates of Parliament (Hansard) to help with understanding the purpose of an Act
      b. Before 1992, this was not allowed.
          - *Beswick v Beswick* [1968] AC 58 'For purely practical reasons we do not permit debates in either House to be cited. It would add greatly to the time and expense involved in preparing cases ... moreover, in a very large proportion of cases [Hansard] would throw no light on the question before the court."
      c. *Pepper v Hart* [1993] 1 All ER 42 - the purposive approach was assisted by being able to consult Hansard, but only where
          - the words of the Act was ambiguous, obscure, or the

literal interpretation led to absurdity
- the words of the Act relied on statements of someone in Parliament
- The Hansard statements were clear
 ii. Royal Commission, etc.
  a. Can be used to help determine the nature of the problem the Act intended to remedy, but not the nature of the solution adopted by Parliament
 iii. Other
  a. International treaties, other Acts, dictionaries, etc.

6. Influence of he EU

6.1. Continental Interpretation
 i. Often have written constitutions
 ii. Substantive law is found in written codes using general language,
 iii. Judges interpret codes to apply to each situation, 'fill in the gaps', free to depart from wording to uphold principles in the constitution
 iv. CJEU draws on the continental tradition
 v. Teleological approach: judges decide a case based on an interpretation of the code that fits with the general intentions of the constitutional principles

6.2. Law of the EU
 i. s.2(4) European Communities Act 1972 - English law is to be interpreted with the principle that EU law stands above it.
 ii. If not, then the English law should not be applied. *R v Secretary of State for Transport, ex p Factortame (No 2)* [1991] 1 All ER 70, HL/ECJ
 iii. On the approach of the CJEU, see *Van Gend en Loos* [1963]: 'To ascertain whether the provisions of an international treaty extend so far in their effects it is necessary to consider the spirit, the general scheme and the wording of those provisions.'
 iv. 'The object of all interpretation lies in the true intention of the lawmakers, whether they be framers of a constitution or a treaty, legislators, or drafters of secondary legislation. Its pursuit at the Court [CJEU] demands of the common lawyer a readiness to set sail from the secure anchorage and protected haven of 'plain words' and to explore the wider seas of purpose and context.' (Fennelly, 'Legal interpretation

at the European Court of Justice' (1996) 20(3) *Fordham International Law Journal*

v. *H P Bulmer Ltd v J Bollinger SA* [1974] Ch 401 (CA), Lord Denning wrote that the literal approach was inadequate dealing with Treaty of Rome because so broadly worded. Clarify by secondary legislation to fill in gaps

    a. All courts should interpret EC law in the same manner and using the same principles

    b. English Statutes are usually specific, and a literal interpretation is common

    c. EC Treaty, in contrast, consists of general principles, aims, and purposes. Gaps exist for the judiciary to fill in

    d. English Courts should use the continental approach when dealing with those rules.

vi. *Buchanan and Co Ltd v Babco Forwarding and Shipping (UK) Ltd* [1977] 2 WLR 107 (CA), Denning argued that the Continental method should be adopted; it is looking to the spirit of the law rather than the letter.

vii. The modern purpose approach is more in line with this than the traditional literal integration of the common law.

viii. Examples:

    a. *Garland v British Rail Engineering Ltd* [1982], HL — held that Sexual Discrimination Act s.6(4) should be interpreted in such a way as to make it consistent with Article 119 of the EEC Treaty; words were capable of two different interpretations; RULE: a statute passed after an international Treaty had to be interpreted as consistent with the obligations that the country had undertaken. (did not address how a statute that intended to contravene a treaty would be interpreted)

    b. *Duke v GEC Reliance* [1998], HL — interpreted Sexual Discrimination Act 1975 s2(4), (6) was not meant to give effect to the Directive on Equal Treatment 1976. s.2(4) did not allow the court to 'distort' the meaning of the statute; but court followed Marshall [1986] which allowed narrower approach: if statute did not intend to give effect to EU obligations, the court was limited, court stayed with literal words of Act. Did not have retrospective act, could not apply. Some interpreters consider this wrongly decided.

    c. In *Marleasing* [1992] the ECJ relied on *Van Colson*

[1983]: a court must interpret national law to be consistent with EU obligations whether or not the national law pre- or post- dated a directive.

d. *Pickstone v Freemans plc* — court approached with far more robustly. HL interpreted Equal Pay Act 1970, amended to make it more in line with Treaty of Rome Article 119; used purposive interpretation unless Act made prior to EU expressly stated allowed it would NOT be intended; court would depart widely from the wording in order to achieve consistency.

e. *Litster and Others v Forth Dry Dock & Engineering Co Ltd* — HL went even further than *Pickstone*; have purposive interpretation to statutory instrument; implied words into the terms of regulation to make it compatible with EU Law; based on determination of the nature of the wordings in both, and it can be 'reasonably construed, then court can imply.

f. Yet literal interpretation is not dead; it is the starting point: *Carole Louise Webb v EMO Air Cargo (UK) Ltd No. 2* and the Sexual Discrimination Act 1975; no need to distort or alter literal sense.

g. Law of EU itself limits purposive approach: *Grant v South Western Trains* [1988]; community law did not recognize homosexual marriages therefore can be dealt with by national law.

7. Human Rights Act 1998

7.1. Introduction

i. Historically, human rights have been of the negative type: whatever is not forbidden is allowed.

ii. Likewise, the common law constrained government power: no one was beyond the law

iii. Access to the courts is also a part of citizen's rights. (See, for example, *R v Lord Chancellor ex p Witham* [1998] QB 575.)

7.2. Domestic Law After HRA 1998

i. Before HRA 1998, courts were only required consider Convention rights in interpreting legislation.

ii. After HRA 1998, the courts are required to do so.

a. Rule of construction applies to past and future legislation

b. s.3(1) HRA 1998 — So far as it is possible to do so, primary legislation and subordinate legislation must be read and given effect in a way which is compatible with the Convention rights.

    c. s.3(2) HRA 1998 — provides that the previous section does not affect any incompatible primary or delegated (secondary) legislation

      - "the role of the court is not (as in traditional statutory interpretation) to find the true meaning of the provision, but to find (if possible) the meaning which best accords with Convention rights." (Lord Hester and Lord Pannick)

7.3. Declarations of Incompatibility

  i. If a court cannot find a way to interpret legislation and remain compatible with the ECHR, then it can issue a 'declaration of incompatibility.'

    a. "If the court is satisfied that the provision is incompatible with a Convention right, it may make a declaration of that incompatibility.: (s.4(1) HRA 1998)

  ii. The option is intended as a last resort.

  iii. The option does not invalidate the legislation and has no effect on cases where such a declaration is made (this is unlike the US Supreme Court, which can declare a law "unconstitutional' and therefore invalid) —this preserves the doctrine of Parliamentary Sovereignty.

  iv. Parliament can, however, amend or repeal the provision in question (s.10 HTA 1998)

7.4. Approach of Courts

7.5. In addition to the other methods of legislation interpretation mentioned above, the courts can employ three others in their attempt to read a provision as compatible with the ECHR

  i. Reading Down — limit the meaning of words

  ii. Reading In — read words or meninges into the legislation

  iii. Reading Out — remove or ignore provisions that cause incompatibility.

7.6. Examples

  i. *R v A (Complainant's Sexual History) sub nom. R v Y (Sexual Offense: Complainant's Sexual History* [2001] 2 WLR 1546

    a. Youth Justice and Criminal Evidence Act 1999 s.41 should be interpreted with 'common sense'

    b. Parliament could not have intended that the Act would prevent an accused from making a full defense; word can be read in; not necessary to issue statement of

incompatibility
  c. Made it compatible with ECHR Article 6(1) [Right to Fair Trial] — but literal interpretation would say complainants must be protected in court concerning sexual history when alleging rape.
7.6.2. *Ghaidan v Godlin-Mendoza* [2004] — Question of succession to a tenancy under Rent Act 1977 ¶2; could be read in a way to make it compliant with ECHR, but new meaning must be 'consistent with the fundamental features of the legislative scheme'
  i. Lord Nicholls noted that there was an ambiguity in the word 'possible' in the HRA s3; NARROW: only allowed courts to resolve ambiguity in favor of convention-compliant interpretations; BROADER: courts can give different meaning to language of statute in order to be consistent with EHCR; no need for language of Act to be ambiguous; can depart from the intention of Parliament
7.7. Declarations of Incompatibility and Government Responses
  i. Since the HRA 1998 came into force, there have been 27 declarations of incompatibility.
  ii. Parliament has no obligation to remedy the incompatibility
  iii. Examples
    a. *R v (1) Mental Health Review Tribunal, North & East London Region (2) Secretary of State for Health ex p H* (2001. The first declaration of incompatibility, issued because two subsections in the Mental health Act 1983 were incompatible with Arts 5(1) and (4) of the ECHR (burden of proof). Parliament amended the Act with the Mental Health Act 1983 (Remedial) Order 2001 (SI 2001/3712),
    b. *Bellinger v Bellinger* [2003] UKHL 21 — Section 11(c) of the Matrimonial Causes Act 1973 declared incompatible with Arts 8 and 12 ECHR. (See *Goodwin v UK* (Application no. 28957/95; 11 July 2002). Parliament remedied this with Gender Recognition Act 2004.
    c. *A v Secretary of State for the Home Department* [2004] UKHL 56. Anti-terrorism, Crime and Security Act 2001 allowed for certified terrorists to be deported but breached Art 3 ECHR. A Derogation Order was used, but quashed because it was not proportionate (as required under Art 15 ECHR). Repealed in Prevention of Terrorism Act 2005.

5. Judiciary

1. Introduction
1.1. "Judges are the very personification of the law. The judicial function embodies the dispassionate application of evenhandedness, integrity, and the rule of law. Judges resolve disputes, punish offenders and, where there is no jury, determine guilt. In the more grandiloquent accounts of law and the legal system, judges are its custodians, guardians of its values: sentinels of justice and fair play ... The role of judges is fundamental to the common law; the centrifugal force of the judicial function drives the legal system both in theory and in practice. And though it may be less significant in the codified systems of Continental Europe, the influence of judges cannot be overstated." (Wacks, 2008)

2. Constitutional Changes
2.1. The rule of law required an independent judiciary, separate from any influence from the executive and legislative
2.2. Before the 18th century, judges could be dismissed at the monarch's desire—they held office *durante bene placito* (at the pleasure of the crown).
2.3. After the English Civil War (1642-1646), changes in Parliament's role, and the Act of Settlement 1701, judges had tenure for life except for misbehavior.

3. Constitutional Reform Act 2005
3.1. Introduced major changes to the judiciary, the final court of appeal, and appointment of judges
3.2. Before the Act
   i. the head of the judiciary was the Lord Chancellor (who also appointed judges)
   ii. position was established 1400 year ago as the secretary to the King, eventually took over other functions, such as presiding over Parliament when the king was absent
   iii. By the 1200s, he was the most senior judge in the end next to the King
   iv. In modern times, the Chancellor as the senior judge, appointment by the current Prime Minister, with a seat in the

cabinet, as well as the Speaker o the House of Lord.

    v. This meant the Chancellor had a role in all three branches of government, normally a red flag for constitutional-based governments.

3.3. After the passing of the HRA 1998, this raised issues of possible conflicts of interest under Art 6 of the ECHR.

    i. "The 1998 Human Rights Act has, of course, invigorated the process of constitutionalisation of public law. The Lord Chancellor is a Cabinet minister. Nevertheless from time to time he sits in the Appellate Committee ... His right to do so is now controversial. Appellate Committees which include the Lord Chancellor may not fulfil the requirement of independence required by Article 6 of the European Convention on Human Rights." (Lord Steyn, 2002)

    ii. This issue was considered by the ECtHR in *McGonnell v UK* [2000], where there was a breach of Art 6 because a bailiff also acted as judge and had also taken an administrative role. The court ruled that even the appearance of partiality must be avoided.

3.4. This led to the passing of the Constitutional Reform Act 2005

    i. Replaced Lord Chancellor as head of judiciary with the Lord Chief Justice

    ii. Established an Independent Judicial Appointments Commission

4. Hierarchy

4.1. Supreme Court Justices (12)

Heads of Division (5)

Lords and Lady Justices of Appeal (35)

High Court judges (108)

Circuit judges (county court and Crown Court) (654)

Recorder (part-time circuit judges) (1196)

District judges (county court and magistrates' courts) Deputy district judges (part-time district judges)

(Tribunals judiciary are based on seniority to court judiciary)

5. Independence of the Judiciary

5.1. Introduction

    i. Independence is ensured by

        a. protection against being dismissed

        b. immunity from legal action

  c. generation pay and employment conditions

 ii. s.3(1) CRA 2005: "The Lord Chancellor, other Ministers of the Crown and all with responsibility for matters relating to the judiciary or otherwise to the administration of justice must uphold the continued independence of the judiciary."

 iii. s.3(5) CRA 2005: "The Lord Chancellor and other Ministers of the Crown must not seek to influence particular judicial decisions through any special access to the judiciary."

5.2. Tenure

 i. high court judges have 'security of tenure during good behaviour'

 ii. Can only be removed from office by both of both Houses of Parliament (no judge has ever been removed in this manner)

 iii. Originally part of there Act of Settlement 1701, now under the Senior Courts Act 1981 and the CRA 2005.

 iv. Judges below this level may be dismissed by the Lord Chief Justice without approval of Parliament (has happened on occasion for incapacity or moral turpitude - usually criminal behavior

 v. For part-time judges, new terms were introduced in 2000; non-renewal of contracts can be for

  a. misbehaviour

  b. incapacity

  c. persistent failure to comply with sitting requirements

  d. failure to comply with training requirements

  e. failure to observe the standards expected from a judge

  f. need to reduce numbers

5.3. Immunity

 i. Cannot be sued for actions or words done in the furtherance of their judicial role in good faith

 ii. This applies to all superior judges, judges of inferior courts, and tribunal judges

 iii. *Sirros v Moore* [1974] 3 All ER 776 - "Ever since the year 1613, if not before, it has been accepted in our law that no action
is maintainable against a judge for anything said or done by him in the exercise of a jurisdiction which belongs to him. The words which he speaks are protected by an absolute privilege. The orders which he gives, and the sentences which he imposes, cannot be made the subject of civil proceedings against him. No matter that the judge was under

some gross error or ignorance, or was actuated by envy, hatred and malice, and all uncharitableness, he is not liable to an action ... Of course if the judge has accepted bribes or been in the least degree corrupt, or has perverted the course of justice, he can be punished in the criminal courts. That apart, however, a judge is not liable to an action for damages. The reason is not because the judge has any privilege to make mistakes or to do wrong. It is so that he should be able to do his duty with complete independence and free from fear." (Lord Denning)

5.4. Salary
  i. judicial salaries should not be reduced during a particular judge's tenure (that is, a judge should be able to rely on the salary offered at the time of appointment, for duration of tenure)
  ii. s.3 Commissions and Salaries of Judges Act 1760, repealed in 1879, and provided in a number of different statutes
      a. salaries and pensions cannot be decreased for office-holders
      b. salaries are paid out of consolidated funds, not the executive
  iii. Reduction of salaries has not been dealt with in England
      a. Ireland amended the Constitution to allow for reduction to keep pace with other public sector offices, but not during a judge's tenure in office
      b. Canada Supreme Court considered the constitutionality of reducing salaries, held it would not be so if for legitimate purposes and part of a general reduction for civil servants. *R v Valente* [1985] 2 SCR 673
  iv. Senior Salaries Review Board reviews salaries for England and Wales annually, makes recommendations to Prime Minister and Lord Chancellor

6. Legitimacy and Authority
  6.1. Impartiality
    i. Old common law principle, *nemo judex in causa sua*: no judge may hear a case in which they have an interest.
    ii. must not only be free from partiality, but even from the appearance of it
    iii. This is because the public must feel it can trust the judiciary
    iv. The test for bias or apparent bias is objective (would a

reasonable and informed outsider, made aware of all facts, believe there could be a case for bias or apparent bias?)

   v. If so, the judge must recuse himself or herself from the case

  vi. See *Magill v Porter* [2001] UKHL 67

6.2. The *Pinochet* case

   i. A coup in Chile in 1973 led by General Pinochet, included terrible acts of violence against citizens, with allegations that the general knew of them

      a. Pinochet came to England for medical treatment in 1998; an extradition warrant was issued by Spain for him

      b. He was arrested under the Extradition Act 1989, but claimed diplomatic immunity

      c. in 1998, a panel of 5 House of Lords judges rejected his claim for immunity

- During the proceedings, Amnesty International made arguments on the case
- It was later discovered that one of the judges, Lord Hoffman, was an unpaid director of Amnesty International and his wife worked for the organization
- Pinochet's lawyers demanded a review by the House of Lords that this constituted a conflict of interest

      d. In 1999, another HoL panel set aside the earlier decision because of Lord Hoffman's involvement (the mere possibility of a conflict of interest was enough)

- the substantive issues of the case would have to be re-heard by a new panel
- The outcome was the same as the first, but for different reasons
- There was speculation as to whether Judge Hoffman would resign because of his failure to disclose, but he did nt

      e. The case established that

- Judges must not only be impartial, they must appear impartial
- Judges are difficult to remove from office, even when they act with serious lapses of judgment such as this

6.3. Recusal from the Court of Appeal before HRTA 1998

   i. *Locabail (UK) Ltd v Bayfield Properties Ltd* [1999] EWCA Civ 3004

      a. CoA held that the relevant test for a conflict of interest or bias set out in *R v Gough (Robert)* [1993] UKHL 1 was for the reviewing court to determine (not the judge in question)

 b. 'In any case giving rise to automatic disqualification ... the judge should recuse himself from the case before any objection is raised. The same course should be followed if, for solid reasons, the judge feels personally embarrassed in hearing the case. In either event it is highly desirable, if extra cost, delay and inconvenience are to be avoided, that the judge should stand down at the earliest possible stage, not waiting until the day of the hearing ... If, in any case not giving rise to automatic disqualification and not causing personal embarrassment to the judge, he or she is or becomes aware of any matter which could arguably be said to give rise to a real danger of bias, it is generally desirable that disclosure should be made to the parties in advance of the hearing. If objection is then made, it will be the duty of the judge to consider the objection and exercise his judgment upon it.' (para.21)

ii. Recusal from HoL after HRA 1998

 a. Since *Locabail* was decided before the HRA 1998, *Director General of Fair Trading v Proprietary Association of Great Britain* [2001] 1 WLR 700 modified the test, which was later affirmed by *Porter v Magill* [2001] UKHL 67:

  - ' 'whether the fair-minded and informed observer, having considered the facts, would conclude that there was a real possibility that the tribunal was biased' (Lord Hope)

7. Appointments before the Constitutional Reform Act 2005

7.1. Appointment

 i. In most common law systems, judges are chosen from legal practitioners who have show integrity and excellent legal skills

 ii. (civil systems choose judges from recent law graduates based on same performance)

 iii. Appointments rarely occurs before age 50 for HC and above

 iv. Judges in England and Wales are refried to as t he 'Queen's judges,' appointed by Her Majesty on advice of ministers

7.2. Importance to the Public

 i. the judiciary suffers a democratic deficit because they are not elected like the other branches

    ii. The public confidence must come from the Judiciary's professionalism and expertise

    iii. 'An essential condition for realizing the judicial role is public confidence in the judge ... [T]he judge has neither sword nor purse. All he has is the public's confidence in him. (Aharon Barak, *The Judge in a Democracy*, Princeton University Press, 2006), 109)

    iv. Since before the 19th century the English judiciary has a reputation for the highest standards

    v. Still, some question the arrangement as it impacts the rule of law. (See, for example, Brian Tamanaha, *On the Rule of Law*, Cambridge University Press, 2004, 125.

7.3. Diversity and Legitimacy

    i. Recent concerns about the judiciary question its composition, which does not reflect society at large or the rest of the legal profession

    ii. 'the first requirement of any institution which exercises legislative power is that it should be representative of those on behalf of whom it exercises that power.' (Ewing, 2001).

    iii. As part of the 2005 reforms, the judicial appointment system was transformed

        a. A new independent judicial appointments commission was created

8. Appointments Before the Constitutional Reform Act 2005

8.1. The Process

    i. Before 1990 appointments were limited to qualified barristers:

        a. Lords of Appeal in Ordinary (Law Lords): 15 years as barrister

        b. Lords Justices of Appeal: 15 years as barrister

        c. High Court judges: 10 years as barrister

        d. Circuit judges: 10 years as barrister or 7 years as recorder

        e. Recorders: 10 years as barrister or solicitor

        f. District judges: 7 years as barrister or solicitor

    ii. After 1990, the Courts and Legal Services Act (CLSA) 1990 was passed

        a. s.119: 'the rights to exercise any of the functions of appearing before and addressing a court including the calling and examining of witnesses.'

        b. Qualifications:

- Lord of Appeal in Ordinary (Law Lords): 15 year Supreme Court Qualification under CLSA of holding of high judicial office for 2 years
- Lord Justice of Appeal: 10 year High Court qualification under CLSA of holding of a post as a High Court judge
- High Court judge: 10 year High Court qualification under CLSA of holding of a post as a circuit judge for 2 years
- Circuit judge: 10 year Crown Court/county court qualification under CLSA or holding of a post as recorder, district judge, tribunal chairman for 3 years
- Recorders: Crown or county court qualification for 10 years
- District judge: General qualification for 7 years

iii. Eligibility was further broadened under the Tribunals, Courts and Enforcement Act (TCE Act) 2007, requiring relevant legal qualification for the specific period, and legal experience while having that qualification

iv. Before the 1990s judicial appointments are made by department

   a. Most were made by invitation and confidential consultations

   b. The lack of transparency was criticized

   c. The organization JUSTICE published a report in 1992

- Qualities and skills required should be established and published
- The pool from which appointments were made should be broader
- The mandatory retirement age should be lowered
- Permanent part-time appointments should be allowed
- The possibility of beginning a judicial career should begin at an earlier stage
- Term appointments should be available at all levels for those who prefer them that

   d. The report also argued for modern appointment procedures to increase diversity

- The use of formal, generally accepted procedures
- A process for developing the careers of junior judges
- And assessment process for judicial posts
- Advocacy should be one of the skills, but not decisive

- Actions to widen opportunities for women and
minorities
e. Many of these improvements were made in the 1990s
8.2. Peach Report on Judicial Appointments 1999
i. An independent report on judicial appointments by Sir
Leonard Peach
ii. He concluded the process was thorough, competent, and
professional and as good as any in the public sector
iii. He noted that changes that have been made in the recent
decade
iv. He recommended the establishment of a commission for
judicial appointments
a. Monitor procedures
b. Act as ombudsman for complaints
c. No role in the actual appointments
8.3. Commission for Judicial Appointments 2001–2005
i. This commission was established in 2001 for England and
Wales
ii. To hear complaints about the system, audit the process (but
not to appoint judges)
iii. The commissioners identified a number of problems in the
system
iv. Recommended that the commission be dissolved an
independent judicial appointments commission be
established
8.4. Judicial Appointment Process Before 2006
i. The criticisms of lack of transparency and process problems
did not extend to the quality of those who have been appointed
ii. Instead, the criticism was that the group lacked gender, ethnic,
social, and cultural diversity that matched population of
England and Wales and the diversity of practicing barristers
and solicitors
iii. Especially at the senior level, the judiciary was mostly white
males from privileged backgrounds privately educated at
Oxford or Cambridge
iv. In 2004 the first female member was appointed the House of
Lords (Baroness Hale of Richmond — white and educated at
Cambridge)

9. Selection Process After CRA 2005
9.1. Argument for Change by the Government

i. Into thousand and three the Secretary of State for constitutional affairs issued a consultation paper describing the government's purpose in establishing a new independent judicial appointments commission
   a. To reinforce the constitutional separation of powers
   b. To increase the diversity of the judiciary

ii. 'In a modern democratic society it is no longer acceptable for judicial appointments to be entirely in the hands of a Government Minister. For example the judiciary is often involved in adjudicating on the lawfulness of actions of the Executive. And so the appointments system must be, and must be seen to be, independent of Government. It must be transparent. It must be accountable. And it must inspire public confidence.

There is a second point ... the current judiciary is overwhelmingly white, male, and from a narrow social and educational background. To an extent, this reflects the pool of qualified candidates from which judicial appointments are made: intake to the legal professions has, until recently, been dominated by precisely these social groups.

Of course the fundamental principle in appointing judges is and must remain selection on merit. However the Government is committed to opening up the system of appointments, to attract suitably qualified candidates both from a wider range of social backgrounds and from a wider range of legal practice. To do so, and, to create a system which commands the confidence of professionals and the public, and is seen as affording equal opportunities to all suitably qualified applicants, will require fresh approaches and a major re-engineering of the processes for appointment ... Accordingly the Government intends to establish an independent Judicial Appointments Commission to recommend candidates for appointment as judges on a more transparent basis.'

iii. The CRA 2005 establish this judicial appointments commission
   a. The commission makes recommendations
   b. The government minister has approval and veto power
   c. The senior judiciary has influence

iv. The Crime and Courts Act 2013:
   a. The minister and Lord Chancellor make appointments to the High Court and above

        b. The Lord chief justice makes appointments below that level
        c. The senior president of tribunals makes appointments to tribunals

9.2. Judicial Appointments Commission
    i. Responsible for candidates to the High Court and and all courts In tribunals below
    ii. Is involved in the appointments to Courts of Appeals, heads of division, and Supreme Court
    iii. Made up of five judicial members, two professional members, five laypeople, one tribunal judge, one lane magistrate
    iv. The commissions obligations
        a. Selections are made solely on merit
        b. Selections are only people of good character
        c. The commission should have regard for the need of diversity (the commission was not required to increase the diversity but widen the pool of candidates available)

9.3. Appointment on Merit
    i. Intellectual capacity
    ii. Personal qualities
    iii. The ability to understand and deal fairly
    iv. Exhibit authority and communication
    v. Exhibit leadership and management skills

9.4. The Process
    i. Includes:
        a. application forms and references
        b. Short listing and a possible test
        c. Interviews with candidates
        d. Role playing
        e. Statutory consultation
        f. Character background checks
    ii. Once these are completed Report is made to either the Lord Chancellor, The Lord Chief Justice, or the senior president of tribunals depending on the appointment level
    iii. Objectives
        a. Modernize the process
        b. Broaden the pool of candidates
        c. Establish a program of education and publicity of the work of the Commission
        d. Dispel myths about judicial appointments

    e. Encourage underrepresented qualified candidates
  iv. Its success in the last Objective has been criticized from the start

10. Increasing Diversity

10.1. Introduction

i. Traditionally, the composition of the judiciary reflected the composition of the bar which was mostly male and white.

ii. The last decades there is been attempts to make the judiciary reflect the composition of the population

iii. After 25 years of addressing the situation, Lord chief justice Taylor's comments in 1992 have not been realized to the extent he predicted

    a. 'The present imbalance between male and female, white and black in the judiciary is obvious ... I have no doubt that the balance will be redressed in the next few years ... Within five years I would expect to see a substantial number of appointments from both these groups.' (The Richard Dimbleby Lecture 1992)

10.2. Why does it matter?

i. The 2004 paper 'Increasing diversity in the judiciary' by the Department for Constitutional Affairs, described the reason why the government thought the change in the judiciary mattered:

    a. 'Society must have confidence that the judiciary has a real understanding of the problems facing people from all sectors of society ... If the make-up of the judiciary is not reflective of the diversity of the nation, people may question whether judges are able fully to appreciate the circumstances in which people of different backgrounds find themselves ... We must ensure that our judicial system benefits from the talents of the widest possible range of individuals in fairness to all potential applicants and to ensure that talent, wherever it is, is able to be appointed.'

ii. Since then, Arguments have coalesced around three topics"

    a. Equal opportunities for all qualified people on the merits without regard to gender, skin color, ethnic origin, class, sexuality, disability, etc.

    b. The legitimacy of the judiciary is hurt by a lack of diversity because of the power that an elected group has if

it's composition does not reflect society as a whole
- 'diversity in senior judicial appointments is not simply a desirable goal, but a fundamental constitutional principle. At the very heart of the legitimacy of an independent judiciary are its claims to be able to deliver 'fairness'. A senior judiciary whose composition reflects an apparent lack of fairness runs the real risk of undermining its own authority.' Paterson and Paterson (2012)
- 'In a democracy governed by the people and not by an absolute monarch or even an aristocratic ruling class, the judiciary should reflect the whole community, not just a small section of it.' (Lady Hale, 'Women in the judiciary', Fiona Woolf Annual Lecture, June 2014)
c. Of varied and wider composition of the judiciary Will bring broader perspectives to the legal issues addressed
- Since the decisions of the courts Will impact all areas of society at sometime, a judiciary that brings background from all those areas Will be more just

10.3. Progress
i. The JAC strategy consisted of three elements
a. Make the process fair and non-discriminatory
b. advertising and outreach to encourage wide pool of candidates
c. work with other organizations to remove barriers to wide pool of candidates
ii. Number of women appointed to judiciary has increased, other areas have not grown as expected
iii. April 2009: the Lord Chancellor to set up an Advisory Panel on Judicial Diversity, chaired by Baroness Neuberger
a. 'to identify the barriers to progress on judicial diversity and to make recommendations to the Lord Chancellor on how to make speedier and sustained progress to a more diverse judiciary at every level and in all courts in England and Wales.'
b. The Panel suggested 53 measures to increase diversity, which were accepted by the Lord Chief Justice
iv. May 2011: House of Lords Constitution Committee instituted a further inquiry into appointments
a. Is the appointment process fair, independent, and transparent?

b. Does the process results in an independent judiciary?
c. Are the candidates appointed on merit?
d. Is the judiciary as diverse as it should be?

v. 2012 report concluded
   a. The Neuberger Panel recommendations should be implemented more quickly
   b. The judicial appointment selection committee should include laypersons
   c. The judicial appointments committee goal should be extended to the Lord Chancellor and order Chief Justice
   d. s.159 of the Equality Act 2010 should be part of the appointment process ('tipping provision')
   e. Within five years, if there is no significant increase in the goals, the government should consider Setting targets (non-mandatory)

vi. Some of the suggested changes were introduced into the Crime and Courts Act 2013
   a. The Lord chief justice makes appointments directly you lower the level of high court (Rather than the Lord Chancellor)
   b. The senior president of tribunals makes appointments to tribunals
   c. Senior judges may not participate in the process to select their own successors
   d. Work patterns for the High Court and above are more flexible

vii. Dec 2014: statistics of the judicial appointment commission show the number of women has increased, the number of black and minority ethnic lawyers what is still low and perhaps decreasing

10.4. Crime and Courts Act 2013 (equal merit provision or 'tipping' provision

i. Amended to the CRA 2005 provides that, when there are two or more candidates of 'equal merit,' the final candidate may be chose for the purpose of increasing diversity.
ii. The provision can be applied only at the final decision stage
iii. Only where the remaining candidates are of equal merit
iv. Only in respect to gender or race
v. This provision has been controversial
   a. some women and minorities believe being appointed under such a condition would undermine the position as a

        judge (chosen on the basis of race or gender)

    b. Others doubt it will make much of a difference because they believe situations in which the provision would apply would be rare

10.5. Reasons for lack of progress

  i. Experience

    a. There appears to be a lack of qualified women and minorities; even if the process is fair or 'tipped,' if there are no qualified candidates, the process will have no effect

    b. Lord Sumption was opposed to positive discrimination because he thought it would actually discourage applications on the basis of undermining their qualifications

      - His suggestion was to encourage women and minorities at the lower levels of education and opportunity, and that, over time, this would increase the number of women and minority candidates for the top positions

    c. Lady Hale questioned some of this because of the slow progress being made

      - 'So do we need to revive the argument for some special provision ... to enable the appointing commissions to take racial or gender balance into account when making their appointments? Would that really be such a bad thing?' (Speech on Equality, 2013)

  ii. Self-exclusion

    a. Under-represented groups are not attracted to judicial appointments or lack confidence to embark upon that path

    b. 2008 Genn research showed that some practitioners do not apply for various reasons (doubt they have the temperament, do not think they would enjoy it, loss of flexibility and autonomy, male-dominated profession is a negative for some women

  iii. Bias

    a. Those who select candidates may be 'self-replicating,' i.e., choose candidates that are like themselves because they identify with them.

    b. This might cause them to overvalue some characteristics and undervalue others out of familiarity.

  iv. Merit

    a. The concept that one person out of a pool is the best

option can be questioned
- It may be the case that a number of final candidates are of equal merit
- The need to choose 'one' causes selectors to make finer and finer distinctions that may be based on familiarity (bias) that does not lead to diversity
- 'I have only one problem about the merit criterion. It is often deployed by people who, when you scratch the surface, are really talking about 'chaps like us.' That is the danger of merit. Who defines it?' (Lord McNally, to the Lords Constitution Committee Inquiry on Judicial Appointments)
- 'The relentless focus on one (flawed) construction of perceived individual merit must move towards a process in which the needs of the judiciary as a collective institution are central. It is in relation to this that the consideration of the constitutional rationale for a diverse judiciary becomes crucial.' (Paterson and Paterson (2012), 48.
- The Bindman and Monaghan 2014 report, *Judicial diversity: accelerating change*, recommended diversity quotas but as of May 2015, it is not clear whether the recommendation will be implemented.

11. Judicial Power and Relationship to the Executive and Legislative

11.1. Judicial power in most common law systems has grown since WWII. Friedman Goldstein, 2004, describe this as a shift from democracy to 'juristocracy'

11.2. Some in the UK argue this has shifted the balance of power in the UK

11.3. Vernon Bogdanor, leading political scientist, argued the following reasons for this shift (2006):
 i. Public discontent and lack of trust in politicians
 ii. The trust of judicial review of the political system
 iii. Increasing emphasis on human rights as a result of multiculturalism
 iv. A more developed sense of rights among citizens
 v. Membership in the EU which affected domestic law (i.e., the *Factortame* and other cases)
 vi. Devolution in the United Kingdom which increases the role

        of courts

11.4. Bogdanor said this shift has happened far more rapidly in the UK then in the US

    i. 'We are now however looking increasingly to judges and not to Parliament to

      guarantee our rights. We are looking increasingly to judges and not to Parliament to check the executive. We are looking increasingly to judges and not to Parliament to determine the division of power between Parliament and the European Union, and between Parliament and the devolved bodies. The judiciary therefore is becoming a more important part of our constitution. We are engaged, it seems to me, in a quiet but nevertheless profound constitutional revolution.'

    ii. More and more often, judges are making decisions that politicians use to make

    iii. These decisions are often political rather than legal

11.5. Advances in technology have led to ethical challenges are new to the world

    i. Life and death, abortion, privacy, etc.

    ii. Example: *Re A (Children)* [2000] EWCA Civ 254 — 'In the past decade an increasing number of cases have come before the courts where the decision whether or not to permit or to refuse medical treatment can be a matter of life and death for the patient. I have been involved in a number of them. They are always anxious decisions to make but they are invariably eventually made with the conviction that there is only one right answer and that the court has given it.'

12. Protection of Human Rights

12.1. HRA 1998 provided that courts and tribunals must take into account ECtHR case law when applicable in deciding domestic cases (s.2 HRA 1998) and must be interpreted in light of the ECHR where 'possible' (s.3)

12.2. Where the application of ECtHR law creates a conflict with a domestic law, the higher courts can declare that it is incompatible with the convention (s.4 HRA 1998)

12.3. All public bodies except Parliament have the duty to function within convention rights unless excluded specifically by primary legislation (s.6 HRA 1998)

12.4. This has created a shift in the balance of power and tensions between the executive, legislative, and courts

12.5. This has led to increasing calls for Britain to exit the EU, which has led to the United Kingdom European Union membership referendum to be held on 23 June 2016.

13. Terrorism

13.1. In recent years, there has been much criticism in relationship to how the courts have dealt with terrorism and security

13.2. Anti-Terrorism, Crime and Security Act of 2001

    i. *A and X v Secretary of State for the Home Department* [2004] UKHL 56 (the *Belmarsh* case) — under the Act, 9 foreigners were detained without trial for over 3 years. The detainment was challenged, and the House of Lords held it to be unlawful and incompatible with the ECHR (which they were required to do under HRA 1998). The popular press criticized the high court for overriding legislation that was designed to protect the country and passed by elected officials.

    ii. The Government repealed the ACSA and passed a new Act, the Prevention of Terrorism Act 2005

13.3. Closed proceedings and the principle of openness

    i. *Al Rawi v The Security Service* [2011] UKSC 34 — The issue before the court had to do with compensation four mist treatment of suspected terrorists; specifically whether the court had the power to allow the defendant to exclude certain material from trial where it might be contrary to the public interest. The high court granted that it could be so in a civil claim for damages; the Court of Appeal disagreed; the Supreme Court dismissed the appeal.

    ii. "There are certain features of a common law trial which are fundamental to our system of justice (both criminal and civil) ... trials should be conducted and judgments given in public ... The open justice principle is not a mere procedural rule. It is a fundamental common law principle." (Lord Dyson)

    iii. After the case, parliament passed the Justice and Security Act (JSA) 2013 to allow such in civil proceedings. The act has been controversial and there was much opposition

        a. 'Secret trials undermine the principles of open justice and natural justice on which the rule of law is built.' (Barrister Michael Fordham)

13.4. Prisoner voting rights

    i. This was another area in which the government was opposed to a new law despite the ruling by courts.

    ii. In *Hirst (No 2) v UK* (2005), *Greens v UK* (2010) and
        Scoppola v Italy (2012)) the ECtHR held that day General
        prohibition against prisoners voting is incompatible with
        Article 3 of protocol No 1

    iii. *R (on the application of Chester) v Secretary of State for*
        Justice [2013] UKSC 63 — a prisoner with a life sentence
        claims that his rights we're denied because he was not
        allowed to vote. The high court and Court of Appeal held
        that it was not the role of the court to implement the ruling in
        Hirst (No 2). The issues for the Supreme Court were whether
        Hirst (No 2). should be applied and if the current rule law
        violated A3P1. The court ruled that under HRA 1998 they
        were required to take into account the decisions of the
        ECtHR but not necessarily to follow them. But since the
        ECtHR had ruled twice on this issue, the court followed
        Hirst (No 2) but did not issue a declaration of incompatibility
        since it was already under review by Parliament.

    iv. Government drafted the Voting Eligibility (Prisoners) Draft
        Bill in Nov 2012, which has been the subject of much debate
        and has still not gone to final vote as of Feb 2016.

13.5. Does HRA 1998 give too much power to the judiciary?

    i. Some have argued that the effect of ECHR and ECtHR case
      law has

        a. removed sentencing discretion from the executive branch
        b. Lifted the ban on homosexuals in the Armed Forces
        c. Ended detention without trial of suspected foreign
           terrorists
        d. Preventing deportation of foreigners who might face real
           risk of inhumane treatment

    ii. 'The domestic effects of decisions reached in some of these
        areas may sometimes pinch, but it is difficult to regard it as
        unforeseeable that a court, established by consent of European
        states to give effect to the Convention, should reach them.'
        (Lord Mance (2013)

6. Civil Justice System

1. Introduction

1.1. In contrast to the criminal system, the civil system provides a process for individuals and organizations to resolve legal disputes

1.2. (not to be confused with a civil legal system in contrast to a common law system)

1.3. The body of legal rules is different for the civil system then it is for the criminal system

   i. The agencies and professionals involved are also different

   ii. The burden of proof and standard of proof are also different

1.4. The state is not a party to civil lawsuits, it is between individuals, Organizations, or a combination

1.5. The laws in issue are passed by the legislature, or developed through the court system and precedent

1.6. There are a number of public and private dispute resolution processes available to avoid going to court

2. Civil v Criminal

2.1. The purpose of civil justice is usually redress, As opposed to criminal justice which is punishment

2.2. Who initiates

   i. The person who has suffered a wrong becomes the claimant

   ii. The person against him the cases brought is the defendant or respondent

2.3. Burden and standard of proof

   i. The responsibility proof is on the person who initiates the case, The claimant

   ii. The standard of proof is on the balance of probabilities, that is it is more likely than not that the defendant is liable (less demanding than the criminal Standard of proof)

2.4. Most civil cases are decided by judges or magistrates, rarely by Juries

2.5. Penalties

   i. In several cases a defendant who is found liable for a wrong is required to fulfill the remedy ordered by the court

    a. Financial compensation
    b. Injunction or declaration
    c. Other

3. Scope

3.1. The civil justice system is more broad and complex than the criminal system

    i. The range of claimants and defendants is broad: individuals, groups of individuals, businesses, and other organizations the state itself

    ii. The areas of law are broad: tort, land, landlord and tenant, family, administrative, company, commercial, employment, and more

    iii. 'the parts of the legal system that are not concerned with criminal law comprise a rag-bag of matters and participants. There are disputes relating to the performance or non-performance of contracts involving businessmen suing each other, individuals suing businesses, and businesses suing individuals. There are claims for compensation resulting from accidental injury in which individuals sue institutions. There is the use of the courts by lenders who realize their security by evicting individual mortgage defaulters. Civil justice also involves attempts by citizens to challenge decisions of central and local government bureaucrats, a rapidly growing field that includes immigration, housing, mental health, child welfare, and the like. In these situations individuals and groups confront agencies of the state which can bring to bear apparently unlimited resources to ward off claims. Finally, there are the acrimonious and often heart-breaking struggles between men and women following the breakdown of family relationships as property and children become the subject of legal dispute. All of these matters come within the ambit of the civil justice system.' (Genn, 'Understanding civil justice' (1997) 50(1) *Current Legal Problems*, 160).

    iv. This complexity makes it is difficult to generalize about civil law, and makes reform difficult

    v. The goals of accessibility, affordability, efficiency, fairness, injustice, can be difficult because of the complexity

    vi. Public courts set up and run by the state apply for the common law and statutes for citizens

    vii. Private dispute resolution (ADR) options are also available
- a. Arbitration has being used for many decades to resolve commercial and other disputes
- b. Mediation options are more recent
- c. Such resolution processes are private and confidential (see below)

4. Public Good

  4.1. Introduction
- i. A civil justice system provides an orderly process for disputes between citizens and organizations
- ii. It has a dispute resolution options to avoid high costs of litigation
- iii. It's supports social order and economic activity
- iv. It provides citizens without process to enforce governmental duties and a check on the misuse of power
- v. Publicity of proceedings and adjudication
  - a. When cases are adjudicated by the judges, a public Record of how courts interpret the law is available to all
  - b. This ensures that individuals and organizations can know the law
  - c. 'Where there is no publicity there is no justice. Publicity is the very soul of justice. It is the keenest spur to exertion, and the surest of all guards against improbity. It keeps the judge himself, while trying, under trial.' (Jeremy Bentham)
  - d. Of course, private dispute resolution processes that are confidential do not have these benefits.

  4.2. Process
- i. Most disputes, especially contracts or commercial or consumer transactions, Are settled by direct negotiation between the parties
- ii. Dispute resolution, Arbitration, and mediation are available when the third party is needed to resolve the dispute
- iii. If these options do not result in a solution, or if a defendant is unwilling to address the dispute, the court has the power to compel and decide the case
- iv. The court system and the process have a clear structure
  - a. The process is referred to as litigation; the parties are litigants
  - b. The Issue of Proceedings is the beginning of a civil court

case where the claimant spells out there case and there proposed remedy

c. The defendant must respond with their defense as to why the claimant is required

d. The court then assigns the case to one of three tracks (See below)

e. The parties prepare their case for trial

f. The case is heard at trial or at hearing, where each side presents evidence, the decision is made, and the remedy is specified

4.3. Settlements

i. Parties can continue to negotiate even after court proceedings have begun

ii. Most cases are settled before trial (usually through the parties attorneys at this stage)

iii. Sometimes even the filing of the issue of proceedings is enough to get a defendant to negotiate in good faith

4.4. Civil Justice and Rule of Law

i. 'In a rule of law society, ordinary people should be able to resolve their grievances and obtain remedies in conformity with fundamental rights through formal institutions of justice in a peaceful and effective manner, rather than resorting to violence or self-help.' (World Justice Project)

ii. The W JP regards the following as necessary for a proper civil justice system

a. Accessibility

b. Affordability

c. Effectiveness

d. Impartiality

e. Cultural competence

iii. Few countries meet all of these expectations (the UK ranks 14th)

iv. 'All around the world, people's ability to use legal channels to resolve their disputes is often impeded by obstacles in judicial decision making, or simply lack of knowledge, disempowerment, and exclusion. These problems, which are not restricted to developing countries, call for more work to ensure that all people have the opportunity to resolve their grievances effectively, impartially and efficiently through the civil justice system.' (WJP)

4.5. Accessibility

    i. Citizens and businesses should be aware of rights, entitlements, obligations, responsibilities

    ii. Citizens and businesses should be aware of options for dispute resolution concerning legal rights, entitlements, responsibilities

    iii. Accessibility to the system, the process, and ability to present the legal merits of the case

    iv. Barriers to these options

        a. Not being aware of rights

        b. Unaware of where to find advice and assistance

        c. Inability to pay for professional representation

        d. Inability to understand a complex legal system

4.6. Access to civil justice and legal aid

    i. One of the tenants of the rule of law is that citizens know their rights and can access the justice system

    ii. Legal services are expensive, in one way to make it accessible for those without funds is to provide a legal aid

    iii. The Legal Aid and Advice Act 1949

        a. 'legal advice for those of slender means and resources, so that no one will be financially unable to prosecute adjusting reasonable claim or defend a legal right'

        b. It became one of the most developed in the world and covered civil, criminal, for all corks through the House of Lords and Supreme Court

        c. In the 1990s it was expanded to include not-for-profit advice agencies and loss centers

    iv. By the mid 1990s the cost of the system was about 2 billion

        a. Most of this was for criminal cases, but much was also for civil, Family, and disputes with the government

        b. The scope has been reduced since then especially for civil and family cases

    v. The Legal Aid, Sentencing and Punishment of Offenders Act 2012 removed legal aid for almost all of civil and family cases

        a. Many criticized this because a lot of the most vulnerable groups in society were affected

        b. People with debt, Benefits, employee, and family problems were affected

        c. Services and advice centers were closed

    vi. November 2014: the national art office produced a report 'implementing the forms to civil legal aid'

        a. Noted that the goal of reducing the amount of money

spent on civil legal aid would be met
   b. Noted that the impact of the changes had not been
      considered by the Ministry of Justice
vii. March 2015: the House of Commons justice committee
     released the results of an inquiry to examine the changes in
     civil legal aid
   a. The inquiry examined the following
      - The effects of the Legal Aid, Sentencing and
        Punishment of Offenders Act 2012
      - Which areas of law and litigants were significantly
        impacted
      - Trends in legally aided civil law cases
      - Whether the Act reduced the money spent as predicted
      - The effects of changes on practitioners and not for
        profit providers
      - The effects of the Act on cases by litigants-in-person
   b. The conclusions were critical of the Act because it failed
      to meet three of its 4 key objectives:
      - Reduce unnecessary litigation
      - Direct legal aid at the most vulnerable
      - Significantly reduce the cost of the system
      - Provide better value for the taxpayers
   c. The Act Head reduced the cost of the system, but failed to
      meet the other three objectives
   d. The report concluded
      - The ministry was not able to ensure that all who are
        eligible were able to access legal aid
      - The Act lead to cutting or downsizing in the legal aid
        market and publicly funded services, leading to
        concerns about the sustainability of the entire system
      - Cases by litigants-in-person had increased
        substantially, which results in more time and expense
        to the courts and assistance to them
      - There had been a significant decrease in the use of
        mediation, The opposite of what had been predicted
4.7. Should there be a right to civil access
   i. The right to access and advise is recognize as part of the rule
      of law, constitutional principles, and also under the common
      law.
   ii. *Witham* [1998] 2 WLR 849
      a. 'It seems to me, from all the authorities to which I have

referred, that the common law

has clearly given special weight to the citizen's right of access to the courts. It has been described as a constitutional right, though the cases do not explain what that means. In this whole argument, nothing to my mind has been shown to displace the proposition that the executive cannot in law abrogate the right of access to justice, unless it is specifically so permitted by Parliament; and this is the meaning of the constitutional right.' (at 585)

   iii. *R (Daly) v Secretary of State for the Home Department* [2001] 2 AC 532
- a. Right of access to courts
- b. right of access to legal advice
- c. Right of confidential communication with a legal advisor

   iv. The right of equal treatment is also recognized by the common law

   v. Art 6(3) HRA 1998 provides the right of legal aid for those accused of criminal wrongs, but this right for civil proceedings is not found in Art 6 ECHR
- a. *Airey v Ireland* 32 Eur Ct HR Ser A (1979): [1979] 2 EHRR 305 considered this issue and held hat the ECHR's purpose was to provide rights for the 'practical and effective' not 'theoretical or illusory', and that legal aid in civil proceedings was not a requirement.

   vi. Some argue that there is a common law right to civil legal aid
- a. 'We do not consider that there is any basis at common law that a litigant is in general entitled to a state subsidy in respect of lawyers' fees. The legal aid reforms do not involve any fundamental right of access to the courts, rather the question of whether a person should receive legal aid funding.' (recent Government comment)

5. Making Civil Justice Accessible

  5.1. Introduction

   i. England has long been concerned about expense, and complexity of the civil system (see Charles Dickens *Bleak House* for a satire of the issue)

   ii. These problems affect common-law civil systems in other jurisdictions as well
- a. The complexity of procedural rules is part of the

adversarial process of the common law
  b. This has to do with procedural fairness in proper notification And ability to prepare for all parties
iii. A balance between these procedures being fair and making the process affordable is necessary
iv. Most agree that simplifying the procedures would result in less cost, and a number of reforms have been attempted

5.2. Woolf Reforms
  i. This review, called access to justice, was by senior judge Lord Wolf, between 1994-1996
  ii. An interim report was released in June 1995, a final report in July1996
    a. New civil procedure rules followed the final report (see below)
  iii. The report argued that the problems of cost, Complexity, and delay were the result of excessively adversarial behaviors by the attorneys
  iv. The solution was to have the courts manage the civil cases
    a. Wolf proposed a system of proportionality
    b. Proposed different civil tracks: simple cases when used quick and clear procedures, The more complicated cases would you use more complex procedures
    c. Proposed the promotion of early settlement, use of the courts should be a last resort
    d. ADR and meditation, private

5.3. Civil Procedure Rules
  i. April 1999
  ii. Designed to be easy to understand (no Latin terms, practice directions, easy-to-follow structure)
  iii. Originally the objective was to 'deal with cases justly'; to emphasize controlling expenses
    a. CPR Part 1.1 'enabling the court to deal with cases justly another proportionate cost'
  iv. Judges manage the cases and encourage cooperation, identifying key issues, encourage settlement through ADR, efficiency
  v. Three procedural tracks
    a. Small claims track (CPR Part 27) - value does not exceed £10,000 (£1,000 for PI and housing); informal, Fast, inexpensive, the court has a lot of procedural leeway
    b. The fast track (CPR Part 28) - value between £10,000 and

25,000; strict timetable, one day trials
    c. The multi-track (CPR Part 29) - all other cases, more complexity, includes pretrial review by the court and active case management

5.4. Legal Costs

    i. Since these reforms, Analysis shows that it has been partially successful in promoting cooperation, settlement, and reducing Delay

    ii. The reforms do not seem to have lowered the costs
        a. In the first three years, costs increased
        b. The rising costs continued through 2008

    iii. Lord Justice Jackson was commissioned to review litigation costs
        a. One of the causes what is the additional work required by the reforms (especially pre-action protocols)
        b. The complexity of the procedure had been increased in some ways, lawyers were required to do more early-stage work, which shifted the time spent do the early part of litigation
        c. Jackson's reforms or implemented in April 2013, but there is controversy over them and whether are they I've made any difference
          - 'The sheer tidal wave of reforms designed to reduce solicitors' costs has also had the effect of reducing access to justice, increasing the number of litigants in person and swelling the already overburdened court waiting lists ...' (The Law Society)

5.5. Increase of Litigants In Person (LIP)

    i. A party has the right in English civil and criminal proceedings to represent themselves in court (this is true of most common law jurisdictions, but not most civil law jurisdictions)
    ii. This is self representation (*pro se* litigation) has increased in common-law jurisdictions around the world
    iii. It especially increased in England after the LASPO 2012
    iv. The cause is the loss of legal aid in the rise and litigation costs

5.6. LIPs that and the adversarial nature of law

    i. Though it is the right, the problem is that adversarial court procedures requires knowledge and training of its complex system
    ii. Research shows that LIPs having difficulty understanding the

law, Collecting evidence, following procedural rules, and are at a disadvantage in arguing their cases

    a. '[LIPs] will not have had the benefit of legal advice to identify the merits and demerits of their proposals ... they will not have had identified to them the issues the court can address before arrival at the court door ... they will arrive without professionally advised applications seeking permission to file evidence ... Many will have no idea what a conventional court process entails and some will have difficulty in understanding its rules.
(Lord Justice Ryder, 'Judicial proposals for the modernisation of family Justice', 2012)

iii. *Re R (A Child)* [2014] EWCA Civ 597 - Lady Justice Black noted that this issue also places an additional burden on the court

iv. The civil justice council recommended simplification of the law, process, and case management (2011)

v. A judicial working group (2013) recommended a more inquisitorial approach for cases involving LIPs

    a. Also recommended greater use of McKenzie Friends (a person who helps an LIP by taking notes, organizing documents, and advising)

5.7. Adversarial v inquisitorial

i. A number of recent cases have discussed the need for flexibility to adapt inquisitorial approaches in cases with LIPs

    a. *Mole v Hunter* [2014] EWHC 658 (QB) - held that courts do have that flexibility

    b. *Re C (A Child)* [2013] EWCA Civ 1412, *Re W (A Child)* [2013] EWCA Civ 1227, *Re D (A Child)* [2014] EWCA Civ 315

        - '... the process of fact finding in family proceedings is quasi-inquisitorial. The welfare of a child may sometimes require a judge to make decisions about facts and/or value judgments that are not asked for by either party. A judge cannot shrink from doing so. That is his function. He must identify such questions and where necessary decide them ...' (Lord Justice Ryder)

ii. President of the family division, Sir James Munby (2014), noted that the current system assumes parties have representation

a. The system will need a radical redesign otherwise
iii. Lord Chief Justice Lord Thomas, in 2014, suggested that inquisitorial approaches were already taking place the family Justice system
iv. The national audit office, *report on implementation of legal aid reforms*, November 2014 found that LIPS:
  a. Less likely to settle
  b. Have more court orders and interventions
  c. Do not have the knowledge and skills to conduct the case efficiently
  d. Caused more work for judges and court staff, which makes the court process inefficient
v. Civil justice council, third for him on litigants in person, December 2014, noted
  a. The need for a coherent strategy
  b. Organizations must collaborate on a system
  c. Paralegals and students could help be part of the solution
  d. Basic assistance is needed to litigants in person
  e. Need to simplify court procedure
  f. Need to train the judiciary

6. Alternative Dispute Resolution

6.1. Introduction
  i. Alternative dispute resolution refers to a number of methods outside of court proceedings
  ii. Negotiation, mediation, conciliation, arbitration, adjudication, early neutral evaluation, ombudsman
  iii. Most of these make use of third party facilitators for settlement
  iv. All are conducted in private, And the results are usually confidential
6.2. Types
  i. Arbitration
    a. an independent third-party (or parties) makes a decision based on the law after hearing both sides presented their case
    b. The decision is known as an award
    c. The decision is legally binding and can be enforced by the courts
    d. Private, confidential
  ii. Early Neutral Evaluation

    a. Each side summarizes their case before a legal professional

    b. The professional offers a nonbinding decision which can then be used as a basis for further negotiations and settlement

    c. Private

iii. Expert Determination

    a. an expert third-party decides the dispute

    b. The decision is binding

    c. Private

iv. Mediation

    a. One of the most popular options

    b. A third party helps two sides reached a settlement (facilitated settlement)

    c. Voluntary and nonbinding, but can be enforced by a contract

    d. The focus is on problem solving rather than strictly Rights under the law

    e. Cheaper and quicker in litigation, flexible, can't apply solutions that could not be done in court, reduces conflict, less stressful than court proceedings, can avoid the adversarial winner and loser approach

v. Conciliation

    a. Similar to mediation, but third party is more active in offering settlement decisions

    b. Often used in employment disputes

vi. Med-Arb

    a. A combination of mediation and arbitration

    b. Begins with a mediated settlement approach

    c. After an agreed-upon time if there is no solution, the mediator arbitrate and make a decision

vii. Ombudsmen

    a. Independent party who investigate and make decisions on complaints by the member of the public about Government departments, Services, in public and private Services

    b. Some use mediation to resolve a dispute

    c. Can award compensation and make recommendations about changes that need to be made to avoid problems in the future

    d. Some of the largest private services are the Financial

Services Ombudsman, Housing Ombudsman, Legal
Ombudsman

6.3. Modern development of mediation

   i. Who some types of arbitration have been used since the 1950s,
the modern techniques came about through the Woolf reports

   ii. Part of this report stress that the courts had a role in both
providing information about ADR and encouraging parties to
engage

     a. '[T]he court will encourage the use of ADR at case
management conferences and pre-trial reviews, and will
take into account whether the parties have unreasonably
refused to try ADR.; (1995 Final Report)

     b. And unreasonable refusal by a party to engage would
allow the court to impose a financial penalty

   iii. Following the report, court based mediation schemes were
established

     a. The court's track and encourage the schemes, but the
mediators were outside trained mediators on a pro bono
basis

     b. This is did not increase voluntary mediation much, but
those who didn't participate reported high satisfaction
with money and time savings

     c. For those that did not result in settlement, costs and time
increased

6.4. The common law and mediation

   i. The voluntary use of mediation between 1996 and 2001 remain
low

   ii. The courts addressed the issue in a number of cases

     a. *Cowl v Plymouth City Council* [2001] EWCA Civ 1935
— parties are required to at least consider ADR where
public money is involved before initiating legal
proceedings

     b. *Dunnett v Railtrack plc* [2002] EWCA Civ 2003 — a
party's refusal to consider mediation before appeal was
enough for legal costs to be denied

     c. *Hurst v Leeming* [2001] EWHC 1051 (Ch) — it is the
judges role to decide whether a parties refusal to mediate
had any justification

     d. *Halsey v Milton Keynes General NHS Trust* [2004]
EWCA (Civ) 576 — if there was no real prospect of a
successful mediation, A party should not be denied legal

costs for refusing. See also *Burchell v Bullard* [2005] EWCA Civ 358

    e. *PGF II SA v OMFS Company* [2012] EWHC 83 (TCC) — if one party refused to except another party's offer of mediation, and the court believes there was a reasonable chance of success in mediation, the court shall consider the refusal in exercising discretion for awarding costs

6.5. Mandatory mediation

    i. The government believes that broader use of mediation schemes Will reduce expenses, the need for legal aid, and court costs and time

    ii. It is promoted as an alternative to court proceedings and is preferred

    iii. The government supports a mandatory mediation System (which has been used for some civil and family cases in Australia and Canada)

    iv. Some members of the Judiciary, legal practitioners, and others are opposed (see Menkel Meadow's arguments)

    v. CPR 26.4

        a. All small claims track court cases are automatically referred to mediation unless there is injection that

        b. It is required in family cases to attend a mandatory information and assessment meeting before being allowed to make some applications to the court

6.6. Evaluating ADR

    i. Positives

        a. Can enable a dispute to end more quickly

        b. Less expensive for the parties

        c. Allows the parties to engage directly rather than through the adversarial process through their attorneys

        d. Some argue that ADR processes increase access to justice

    ii. Negatives

        a. Some research shows that Power imbalances between the parties maybe a disadvantage the the weaker party

        b. The access to justice improvement has been questioned (See Genn, 2009, [age 117)

6.7. Online dispute resolution

    i. February 20 15th report by the Civil Justice Council argued that the goals of accessible affordable justice have not been met

    ii. The report suggested an online court service with a three tier

system
    a. Online dispute avoiding services
    b. Online facilitation to resolve disputes
    c. Online dispute resolution by judges
  iii. 'Firstly, it will increase access to justice because we believe more people will use the system. It will be cheaper, more convenient, less forbidding. And secondly, it will lower the cost to individual participants in disputes and the cost of the overall justice system.' (Professor Richard Susskind, chair of Civil Justice Council Working Group on ODR)
  iv. This proposal is for civil claims under £25,000, But could be extended family disputes and tribunals

7. Trials, Privatization, Rule of Law

7.1. Since the mid-1990s, case is going to trial have decreased dramatically ('the vanishing trial' phenomenon)

7.2. Many common-law jurisdictions around the world have experienced it'

7.3. This seems to be the result other emphasis on dispute resolution, rather than just the expense

7.4. Some have argued that the privatization of civil disputes may lead to the loss of precedent in common-law systems, because private dispute resolution happens outside the system (see Genn (2013))

7.5. Others believe this is simply part of a positive evolution of the Anglo-American system

  i. 'We are now in a time of transition away from trial by the 'ordeal' of court, though it may not be quite clear that we are moving uniformly (or some would argue, returning) toward 'private' trials or other legal events for the resolution of our disputes with each other. I want to lay a more positive cast on the evolutionary story – that the phenomenon of the 'vanishing trial' is not necessarily bad. If litigants and their lawyers are choosing other processes, we must examine why and observe, if we can, the evolutionary picture of why we are moving to new roles and new institutions and what values these new roles and institutions might serve.
(Menkel Meadow, 2012, 87).

7.6. Still, it is true that an increase in pre-litigation settlement, arbitration, and mediation, will have an impact in many areas of law

i. It will lead to a loss of guidance in the law
ii. It will lead to the loss of justice seen by the public
iii. Does this undermine the rule of law principal that legal rules are to be known and adjudicated in public for the continuing good of the system,

7. Criminal Justice System

1. Introduction
    1.1. The line between civil and criminal law is not always a clean line
    1.2. The systems developed over a long period of time with some behavior is regarded as criminal and others as civil
       i. Developing a system from scratch today would probably not result in exactly the same
    1.3. A criminal justice system consists of organizations, agencies, and procedures to prevent, detect, prosecute, and punish actions considered criminal

2. The Criminal Justice System
    2.1. A system of interrelated and interdependent procedures or triggered buy a report of an offense or allegation of an offense
    2.2. There are various stages, in which each stage involves different agencies and persons
    2.3. 'a complex social institution which regulates potential, alleged and actual criminal activity within limits designed to protect people from wrongful treatment and wrongful conviction.' (Sanders, Young and Burton (2010))

3. Purpose
    3.1. Introduction
       i. Auld Review, 2001, identified two main purposes
          a. The reduction of the fear and Social and economic costs of crime, As well as crime itself
          b. The execution of fair and efficient justice to ensure public confidence in law and the system
      ii. 'to deliver justice for all, by convicting and punishing the guilty and helping them to stop offending, while protecting the innocent ... for detecting crime and bringing it to justice; and carrying out the orders of court, such as collecting fines, and supervising community and custodial punishment' (CJS Online, 2010)
      iii. Key purposes
         a. Prevent and deter criminal behavior
         b. Investigation

      c. Evidence gathering

      d. Arresting, charging, prosecuting

      e. Punishment of those found guilty

  iv. Key organizations

      a. The police. Investigate, collect evidence, apprehend suspects, and charge offenses

      b. Crown Prosecution Service. The conduct and process of prosecution

      c. Courts, judges, juries,. Try the accused.

      d. Criminal Cases Review Commission. Deal with miscarriages of justice

3.2. Adversarial System

  i. Evidence-gathering

      a. The parties are responsible for gathering evidence

      b. Evidence is evaluated at trial by a judge or jury

      c. (this is unlike inquisitorial proceedings, where an independent prosecutor or examining magistrate oversee the investigation, seeks evidence, direct lines of inquiry, Interviews witnesses and suspects, and decides whether there is enough to proceed to trial)

  ii. Trial

      a. The parties to determine which witnesses and evidence they will use; the opposing party can cross examine

      b. The court oversees the process to ensure it falls within the rules

        - The rules of evidence are strict against evidence that may prejudice or mislead

      c. The court determines whether there is reasonable doubt or not

      d. (in an inquisitor for proceedings, the the court determines witnesses, order they are heard, and conducts questioning, there is no cross-examination, Fewer rules of evidence

3.3. The Rule of Law

  i. Unlike the civil justice system, the state almost always brings the case against a person or organization

  ii. Since the state has almost unlimited resources for her prosecution, fairness of proceedings is important

      a. Protections against the accused intend to allow adequate opportunity to defend themselves

  iii. World Justice Project is a group which assesses how well countries meet these rule of law standards

    iv. An ideal system investigates and adjudicates criminal
        offenses effectively, impartially, without improper influence,
        insures the rights of suspects and victims
        a. Effective investigation
        b. Timely and effective adjudication
        c. Due process for the accused
        d. Impartiality in the process
        e. Freedom from corruption
        f. Freedom from improper government influence

3.4. How to Evaluate a Criminal Justice System
    i. Different societies approach criminal investigation,
      Prosecution, decision-making differently
    ii. Structures, values, and objections also different
    iii. Even what is considered criminal differs
    iv. To evaluate different systems, Requires an analysis of the
       violence between crime control, rights of the accused, and
       rights of victims

3.5. Crime Control v Due Process
    i. Herbert L Packer's famous two-model analysis the criminal
      justice system (1968): *The limits of the criminal sanction*
      (1968)
        a. Crime control
          - Stopping criminal conduct is the goal
          - Fast and efficient processing
          - High rates of apprehension and conviction
          - Wide powers for police apprehend and investigate
          - Limited opportunities to challenge procedures or
            appeal decisions
          - Rapid assumption of guilt
          - Reliance on investigative skills of police and
            prosecutors
          - Predominant risk of innocent people wrongly
            convicted
          - An 'Assembly line'
        b. Due process
          - Procedure all protections for accused
          - Opportunities to challenge procedures and decisions
          - Extensive rules of evidence, juries, right to remain
            silent
          - Recognition of error in collection of evidence, witness
            memory, coerced testimony

- Predominant risk of guilty people going free
- An 'obstacle course'

ii. William Blackstone, *Commentaries on the laws of England*
— 'the law holds that it is better that
ten guilty persons escape, than that one innocent suffer.'
(1769)

iii. The English system in recent times leans more towards the due process model
  a. HRA 1998 has emphasized this approach
  b. Recent emphasis on the need to control crime especially in relation to terrorism
  c. More current willingness to extend the police powers including electronic surveillance

iv. ECHR articles that have influenced this
  a. Right to a fair trial (Art 6)
  b. Freedom from arbitrary detention (Art 5)
  c. Freedom from inhumane and degrading treatment (Art 3)
  d. Right to privacy (Art 8)

4. Police and Police Powers

4.1. Introduction
  i. Police powers found in Police and Criminal Evidence Act 1984
    a. Codified pre-existing common law and statutes
    b. Stop and search, arrest, search and seizure, detention and questioning, use of evidence
  ii. Includes eight Codes of Practice (s.66) which guide how do power are to be used
  iii. Of breach of any power is a violation of law and can results in civil or criminal Proceedings
  iv. Code of Practice violations may result in the exclusion of evidence (s.78)

4.2. Stop and Search
  i. s.1 PACE gives police Power to stop and search people in public places; must have reasonable grounds for suspicion
  ii. Should be used 'fairly, responsively, and with respect... Without unlawful discrimination'
  iii. Equality and Human Rights Commission report 2010
    a. Blacks were six times more likely to be stopped and searched due to racist views among police
    b. However, Home Office research (2000) showed the

people most likely to be on the streets at night or disproportionately young Black men, Therefore more likely to be stopped and searched
 c. Regardless, public perception is important especially among minority groups
 iv. Police began introducing measures to increased the fairness of stopping search (called 'Plan B')
  a. The stop and search must be proportional in protecting Society and the rights of individual
  b. It must be conducted properly under the law
  c. Recording each incident can lead to accountability
  d. Infringement of rights must be justifiable
  e. Stop and search to be made with the best information reasonably available

4.3. Arrest and Detention
 i. An arrest deprives a person of their liberty under legal authority
  a. *Spicer v Holt* (1977) — ''Whether or not a person has been arrested depends not upon the legality of the arrest, but on whether he has been deprived of his liberty to go where he pleases.'
  b. *R v Lemsatef* [1977] 2 All ER 835 — 'It must be clearly understood that neither customs officers nor police officers have any right to detain somebody for the purposes of getting them to help with their inquiries.'
 ii. s.24 PACE was amended by Serious Organised Crime and Police Act 2005 to allow arrests for
  a. Someone about to commit an offense
  b. Someone in the act of committing an offense
  c. Someone about whom there are reasonable grounds for suspecting to be about to commit an offense
  d. Someone about whom there are reasonable grounds for suspecting in the act of committing an offense
  e. (an officer must tell the person they are in her rest and the reason for it)
 iii. Once arrested, the suspect is taken into a police station before a custody office
  a. Decides whether there is a reason for them to remain
  b. Whether there is sufficient evidence to charge
  c. Most offenses allow maximum of 36 hours without charge
   - A warrant from a magistrate can extend to 96 hours

- The Terrorism Act 2006 allows up to 14 days

5. Crown Prosecution Service
5.1. Introduction
  i. Just because an offender is charged does not necessarily mean they will be prosecuted
  ii. The common law adversarial system requires the prosecution to have a reasonable sense that they can secure a conviction
    a. Otherwise, to put a suspect and victim(s) through the process it is unfair and a waste of public funds
    b. It is the prosecuting Authority who decides whether to proceed on a charge
  iii. Until 1986 police undertook prosecutions in England and Wales
    a. Concerns about fairness, quality of evidence, and bias in favor of guilt led two criticisms
    b. Many cases proceeded with weak evidence
    c. Judges are required to order an acquittal all if they do not believe there is reasonable chance of conviction
    d. *R v Galbraith* [1981] 1 WLR 1039 — 'Where the judge comes to the conclusion that the prosecution evidence, taken at its highest, is such that a jury properly directed could not properly convict upon it, it is his duty, upon a submission being made, to stop the case.'
  iv. Prosecution of Offenses Act 1985 established the Independent Crown Prosecution Service, which took over the functions of criminal proceedings and court prosecution
5.2. Prosecutorial Discretion, CPS Code
  i. Prosecutors have discretion about whether or not to prosecute
    a. The evidence stage
      - Satisfied there is sufficient evidence for the prospect of conviction on each charge
        • The evidence be used in court?
        • Is it reliable?
        • Is it credible?
      - Consider what defense maybe mounted against
      - How likely the prospect of conviction
    b. The public interest stage
      - If a case passes the previous stage, the prosecutors must ask whether it is in the public interest to proceed
        • How serious is it?

- How culpable is the suspect?
- What were the circumstances and harm?
- Was the suspect under the age of 18 when the act was committed?
- What is the impact on society?
- What prosecution be an appropriate response

5.3. Public Interest (e.g., Assisted Suicide)

    i. s.2(1) Suicide Act 1961 allows suicide, but provides for an offense for anyone encouraging or assisting

        a. s.2(4) gives the director of public prosecution's discretion whether prosecute

        b. *R (Purdy) v DPP* [2009] UKHL 45 — the last Supreme Court/House of Lords ruling on the issue

          - 'Consistency of practice is especially important here. The issue is without doubt both sensitive and controversial. Many people view legally assisted suicide as an appalling concept which undermines the fundamental human right to life itself. On the other hand there are those, like Ms. Purdy, who firmly believe that the right to life includes the right to end one's own life when one can still do so with dignity. Crown prosecutors to whom the decision-taking function is delegated need to be given the clearest possible instructions as to the factors which they must have regard to when they are performing it. The police, who exercise an important discretion as to whether or not to bring a case to the attention of the Crown prosecutors, need guidance also if they are to avoid the criticism that their decision-taking is arbitrary. Important too is the general policy of the law that the Attorney General and the Director only intervene to direct a prosecution when they consider it in the public interest to do so.' (para 46)

    ii. January 2010 — Woman acquitted of attempted murder for assisting the suicide of her daughter who suffered from a long-term illness; CPS was criticized for prosecuting under the charge of attempted murder since she had already played guilty to aiding and embedding suicide

    iii. February 2010 — new policy by CPS on prosecution of assisted suicide

        a. '[T]he thrust of the final guidelines is reasonably clear ...

broadly speaking if the victim has a clear and settled intent to commit suicide and if the suspect is wholly motivated by compassion and has not persuaded the victim to commit suicide, the likelihood of a prosecution is low. The guidelines, as I say, have been in force since February 2010 and contrary to views expressed by a number of people they work very well in practice.' (Sir Keir Starmer, LAG Annual Lecture 2013)

iv. *R (on the application of Nicklinson) v Ministry of Justice* [2014] UKSC 38 — request for permission to allow a doctor to help him in his life, died in 2012 pneumonia before the case went to the Supreme Court; his wife continued the case and was joined buy another party requesting the same.

    a. The applicants argued that the policy interfered with article 8 ECHR rights

    b. DPP argued that the policy was clear, and to guarantee it will never prosecute someone for assisting her encouraging suicide would violate 'the line of constitutional propriety.'

    c. The Supreme Court dismissed the appeal, ruling that they did not have jurisdiction to change the law and the DPP's guidelines were lawful

5.4. Evaluating the CPS

i. Since the creation of CPS it has been criticized at various times

ii. Early on it was criticized as being underfunded and not attracting the best

iii. Lord Justice Glidewell Report, 'the review of the crown prosecution service,' reported conflict between the police and CPS, and suggested that putting together in managing case files should be worked on together across agencies

iv. Government White Paper, 'justice for all' (2002) estimated £80 million of waste yearly because of dismissed cases, problem of delays, and 'cracked' trials (where a defendant please guilty the first day of trial)

    a. The Paper attributed these problems to an adequate preparation before trial and Inadequate police files provided to CPS

    b. Recommended the CPS have more responsibility for determining charges

    c. Recommended and improved procedures

    d. Closer work between police and CPS

v. Criminal Justice Act 2003 provided CPS more involvement in prosecutorial decisions and determining the charges

vi. Since these changes, shows an improvement in the CPS's work

6. Courts, Judges, Juries

6.1. Classification of Crimes

i. Summary Offenses — least serious, try in magistrates court's (e.g., driving offenses, minor assault, minor criminal damage)

ii. Triable-Either-Way Offenses — intermediate crimes, Heard in either magistrate court or Crown court's (e.g., theft, assault causing actual bodily harm)

iii. Indictable Offenses — most serious crimes, tried in the Crown Court (e.g., murder, manslaughter, rape)

6.2. Trial and Case Management

i. Overview

a. "the presumption of innocence and a robust adversarial process are essential features of English legal tradition and of the defendant's right to a fair trial' (Lord Chief Justice Woolf, quoted in Ward and Akhtar, 2010, 581)

b. 2001 Review of the Criminal Courts, Sir Robin Auld agreed differently

- 'Procedural fairness has always been a feature of our law. Its articulation as such by our recent adoption of Article 6 adds little of substance to the tradition, though it may generate much litigation on its application in individual circumstances. My main concern here is with the notion of 'balance'. In determining the provision of courts, manner of trial and the search for fair, speedy and otherwise efficient procedures, it should be remembered that they are not there just to protect defendants. They also serve the community. And the criminal process is not a game. It is a search for truth according to law, albeit by an adversarial process in which the prosecution must prove guilt to a heavy standard.' (para 12)

c. In recent years, the government has pressured the criminal courts to increase their efficiency and reduce the cost to the public

d. There are also voices calling for the shift away from Focus on due process to make sure the guilty are not

acquitted wrongly
- 'Justice for All' White Paper argued that the criminal system needed to move more in favor of the victim
- Criminal Just Act 2003 changed some rules of evidence and trial procedures to take away some due process protections that favored defendant

   e. The 2005 Criminal Procedure Rules sought to improve efficiency of trials
- Implemented a new 'overriding objective' that 'criminal cases be dealt with justly,' mirroring the same in the civil procedure rules: all parties are required to prepare and conduct their case following the overriding objective
  - Acquit the innocent, convicted guilty
  - Prosecution and defense treated fairly
  - Recognize defendant rights especially those under article 6 ECHR
  - Keep in mind the interest of witnesses, victims, jurors and keep them informed
  - Be efficient and expeditious in the process
  - Ensure proper information is ready when bail and sentence are considered
  - Take into account the seriousness of offenses, the complexity of matters, consequences to the defendant and others, and the needs of other cases

  ii. Efficiency of the System
    a. Jan 2015, Lord Justice Leveson review of the efficiency of the criminal system, which recommended
- More use of technology, especially to encourage remote hearings
- More efficient case management and the use of timetables
- Use of high quality equipment in court to show footage from body worn police cameras
- Magistrate courts to have more flexible hours for those who cannot attend during normal hours
- Personnel contracts to require more efficiency for those who deliver prisoners to court

6.3. Magistrate Courts
  i. Local courts
  ii. Trials of summary offenses and either way offenses

      iii. No trial by jury, case heard by three justices of the peace
         a. Do not usually have legal qualifications
         b. Part time an unpaid
      iv. District judges are legally qualified and paid
      v. Hear 97% of criminal cases
      vi. Limited sentencing powers, maximum 12 months imprisonment for in offense
      vii. In either way cases, Determine weather the magistrates court should deal with it, or the Crown Court (defendant can choose the Crown Court

6.4. Crown Courts
      i. Located in court centers in England and Wales
      ii. High court judges, circuit judges, recorders
      iii. Can hear all trials for offenses wherever committed
      iv. Unlimited sentencing power
      v. Includes the use of the jury
         a. Listen to evidence
         b. Return a guilty or not guilty verdict (do not have to give reasons
      vi. The judge manages the trial, ensures fairness in evidence, imposes sentences
         a. Must accept the verdict of the jury
         b. In some cases, a judge can deal within offense (see below)

7. Juries

7.1. History
      i. A jury is a group of citizens who hear criminal or civil cases and determine guilt or innocence or liability
      ii. The purpose is to increase citizen participation in the system, encourage impartiality, and encourage public confidence in the system
      iii. Ancient Greece and Rome used citizens to decide criminal offenses in some situations
      iv. The common law practice for criminal cases goes back to the 13th century
         a. It replaced the trial by ordeal
         b. Magna Carta 1215 provided for a person to be tried by 'the lawful judgment of his peers'
      v. Originally, a jury knew the defendant and the accuser, and could provide knowledge and information about the case
      vi. By the 15th century juries were deciding facts and rendering

verdicts
vii. Juries providing verdicts at trials is a feature of common-law systems
    a. In the US, there is a constitutional right to a jury trial
    b. Other common law jurisdictions View it as a privilege and the use of juries is more limited
    c. They are less common in civil law jurisdictions, but the that use of laypersons to help with impartiality and increase public confidence is increasing

7.2. Philosophy
  i. The concept lies in judgment by peers rather than Government or professional judiciary
    a. Judicial function — to decide guilt or innocence based on the evidence only
    b. Social function — provide confidence in the fairness of the system, to allow the citizen a roll in the State's work, to provide a protection against tyranny of the State.
  ii. 'A right to jury trial is granted to criminal defendants in order to prevent oppression by the Government ... Providing an accused with the right to be tried by a jury of his peers gave him an inestimable safeguard against the corrupt or overzealous prosecutor and against the compliant, biased, or eccentric judge. Beyond this, the jury trial provisions in the Federal and State Constitutions reflect a fundamental decision about the exercise of official power – a reluctance to entrust plenary powers over the life and liberty of the citizen to one judge or to a group of judges. Fear of unchecked power, so typical of our State and Federal Governments in other respects, found expression in the criminal law in this insistence upon community participation in the determination of guilt or innocence. (Justice Byron White, US Supreme Court, *Duncan v Louisiana* (1968))
  iii. Article 6 ECHR does not require trial by jury for a fair trial (some believe it should be added)
  iv. Of the jury system note that the ECtHR have found jury selection behavior have violated impartiality and independence

7.3. Juries Use in the Courts
  i. Criminal Trials
    a. Used in the Crown Court on indictment (only 3% of all criminal trials, and most of those plead guilty before)

b. A panel of 12 citizens

c. These cases are usually the most serious and complex and attract the most immediate attention

ii. Civil Trials

    a. Maybe be used in the Queen's bench division of the High Court for defamation, false imprisonment, malicious prosecution by police

    b. A panel of 12 citizens in the High Court, eight in the County Court

    c. The use of juries in civil trials has been decreasing over the last hundred years, rare now

iii. Coroners' Courts

    a. Investigate the cause of death in prison, Police custody, or because of police actions, Industrial and some other accidents

    b. A panel between seven and 11 citizens

iv. Despite the rare use, debate about the use of juries has been vigorous

    a. 'One of the most remarkable aspects of the jury system in England and Wales is that while juries now decide only a small fraction of all criminal cases and almost no civil cases, the right to trial by jury continues to be a highly charged subject. Most discussion of jury policy generates public attention, and virtually every proposal to restrict trial by jury in the last half century has provoked widespread and often impassioned opposition.' (Thomas, 2007, 2).

7.4. Function and Independence

i. To decide matters of fact

ii. The decision is final, and the judge cannot criticize or overturn (*Bushell's Case* (1670) Vaughn 135)

7.5. Verdicts

i. Unanimous verdicts were required until 1967

    a. This resulted in Long deliberation periods in situations where one person could prevent a verdict

    b. If the jury could not reach a unanimous decision, it could be dismissed Anna Reed trial was held

ii. Majority decisions are allowed since 1967

    a. A jury is required to deliberate for two hours, after which if there is no unanimous decision, the judge directs them to come to a majority verdict

b. A full jury of 12 would require 10 or 11 for a proper verdict

c. If the jury has fallen to 11 or 10, then of verdict of 10 or nine is required

d. A jury of nine or less must be unanimous

7.6. Qualifications

   i. Before 1972 a juror had to be a property owner

     a. This led to underrepresentation by women and younger people

   ii. Juries Act 1974

     a. Must be between 18 and 75

     b. Registered to vote

     c. And ordinary resident of UK for minimum of five years since 13th birthday

   iii. A judge may remove a person from jury service if they believe the lack capacity (lack of English skills, a disability)

7.7. Selection

   i. Ideally a representative group of peers

   ii. Selected at random by the Jury Central Summoning Bureau from the electoral register

   iii. A court official chooses from the pool two here particular cases

   iv. They are given an oath, I do not know what trial a serve until sworn in, To avoid prejudgment

7.8. Excusal

   i. Before April 2004 — Doctors, legal professionals, police, and judiciary were automatically excused if they were in eligible or did not want to serve

   ii. The *Criminal Justice Act 2003* abolish the exception

     a. Almost serve unless it causes personal difficulties

     b. One can request excusal, or postponement

     c. The court has discretion whether to grant or not

   iii. The lord Chief Justice issued guidance for judges who serve as jurors

     a. Part of their duty as a private citizen

     b. Only excused in extreme circumstances

     c. Up to the judge to disclose whether he is a member of the judiciary to the jury

   iv. The issue of bias and certain professionals sitting as juries

     a. *R v Abdroikof, R v Green and R v Williamson* [2007] UKHL 37, [2007] 1 WLR 2679 — all involved police

officers were prosecutors serving as a jury member;
majority ruled that the fact of a member of the jury being
such did not make the trial unfair unless the professional
had worked in the same office I someone giving evidence
for the prosecution; also that if I jerk was a local crown
prosecutor in the CPS this would give the appearance of
bias '

b. *Hanif v UK* (2012) — the ECtHR held that there was
violation of Article 6(1) ECHR if police officer as juror
new one of the police witnesses

8. Independence and Impartiality

8.1. Reasons

i. Juries are not required to give their reasons, unlike judges

  a. 'Judges give their reasons, either so as to satisfy the
parties or because they themselves want to justify their
judgments. Even arbitrators detail their findings of fact.
The jury just says yes or no. Indeed, it is not allowed to
expand upon that and its reasons may not be inquired into.
It is the oracle deprived of the right of being ambiguous.
The jury was in its origin as oracular as the ordeal: neither
was conceived in reason: the verdict, no more than the
result of the ordeal, was open to rational criticism. This
immunity has been largely retained and is still an essential
characteristic of the system.' (Lord Devlin, Hamlin
Lectures on the Jury, 1956, 14).

ii. s.8(1) Contempt of Court Act 1981 — no one ask the jury
about their reasons, deliberations are confidential

  a. *Taxquet v Belgium* (2012) 54 EHRR 26 — challenge to
this provision; court held 'the Convention does not require
jurors to give reasons for their decision and that Article 6
does not preclude a defendant from being tried by a lay
jury even where reasons are not given for the verdict.'

iii. *R v Mirza* [2004] UKHL 2 — two questions:

  a. If a jury member gives notice to court that there is reason
to believe bias, does the law allow it to be used as
evidence in appeal,

  b. Is s.8(1) Contempt of Court Act 1981 compatible with
Art 6 ECHR that it prohibits the admission of evidence of
bias?

  c. Majority held that the common law prevails and that the

Act was compatible with Art 6. '[T]he law ... recognises that confidentiality is essential to the proper functioning of the jury process, that there is merit in finality and that jurors must be protected from harassment. These requirements too are directed to the essential object of maintaining public confidence in this mode of trial. So the general rule is that, after the verdict has been returned, evidence as to things said by jurors during their deliberations in private is inadmissible.' (Lord Hope)

   iv. *AG v Scotcher* [2005] UKHL 36, [2005] 1 WLR 1867 — While a jury member can reveal information of deliberations in the belief that there was bias, these concerns must be revealed to the court and not a third party.

   v. Law Commission has recommended that the provision be rewritten to address disclosure to court officials, police, or the criminal cases review commission underbelly that it is necessary to avoid a miscarriage of justice

8.2. Race and Fairness

   i. Many believe that the fairness of the system is compromised if juries do not adequately represent black or minority groups

   ii. *R v Ford* [1989] 3 All ER 445 — judges are not obligated to create multi racial juries

     a. A randomly creates fairness

     b. No principle of law demands racially balanced juries

     c. 'however well-intentioned the judge's motive might be, the judge has no power to influence the composition of the jury and that it is wrong for him to attempt to do so. If it should ever become desirable that the principle of random selection should be altered, that will have to be done by way of statute and cannot be done by any judicial decision.' (Lord Lane)

   iii. Royal Commission on Criminal Justice 1993 (the Runciman Commission) — recommended that either party could insist on up to three ethnic minorities, and one from the same as the accused or victim in exceptional cases; this recommendation was not adopted

   iv. Lord justice Auld review of the criminal courts (2001) — recommended option to select to ethnic minority jurors where race is an issue in the offense; this recommendation was not adopted

   v. Government White Paper 2002 ('Justice for All') — opposed

the selection of multi racial juries
  a. It would undermine randomness and not achieve representation
  b. Would put those specially selected an awkward position
  c. Generate tensions and divisions
  d. Put undo on the views of those special jurors
  e. Place a burden on the court to decide which cases should allow multiracial selection
vi. *R v Smith* [2003] EWCA Crim 283 — on appeal asked if *Ford* was incompatible with Art 6 ECHR; '
    We do not accept that it was unfair for the appellant to be tried by an all-white jury or that the fair-minded and informed observer would regard it as unfair. We do not accept that, on the facts of this case, the trial could only be fair if members of the defendant's race were present on the jury. It was not a case where consideration of the evidence required knowledge of the traditions or social circumstances of a particular racial group. The situation was an all too common one, violence late at night outside a club, and a randomly selected jury was entirely capable of trying the issues fairly and impartially.'
vii. *Sander v UK* [2000] ECHR 194 — held that a fair trial requires impartiality, therefore the make up of a jury could be contested if in doubt
viii. Recent research in jury summoning by Cheryl Thomas (2007) concluded
    a. There is no underrepresentation of black or minorities call to serve
    b. No significant difference between ethnic minorities in white majority and willingness to serve
    c. Subsequent studies (2010) using a large database of verdicts found no evidence of discrimination by all white jerseys, no evidence of stereotyping by jurors, no need to seek enforced mixed juries
ix. Other findings about juries:
x. They are efficient and effective
xi. Once sworn in, 89% reach a verdict by deliberation
xii. Once deliberation begins, juries reach vertex on over 99% of all charges
xiii. Juries convict on 64% of all charges
8.3. Fairness and the Internet

i. Contempt of Court

    a. 'Litigants – and the public – must have confidence that the court's decision will be based only on the evidence which was seen and tested by all parties. The law of contempt of court also aims to ensure that no-one can undermine the functions of the court, either by depriving the court of the ability fairly to decide the case or by hindering the enforcement of the court's judgment.' (Law Commission report)

    b. Art 6 ECHR — a tribunal which tries the case must be independent, impartial
- 'right to be tried according to the evidence properly placed before court, and on that evidence alone'
- Evidence outside of court should have no role or influence

    c. The widespread use and development of the Internet has caused problems in this area

    d. *AG v Dallas* [2012] EWHC 156 (Admin) — unsure sentenced to six months for contempt because she did Internet research on the defendant, and discovered he had previously been convicted of rape; she discussed this material in deliberations; when reported to the judge he discharged to the jury in order to retrial
- 'By [disobeying the judge's order not to look on the internet] she did not merely risk prejudice to the due administration of justice, but she caused prejudice to it. This was because she had sought to arm and had armed herself with information of possible relevance to the trial which, although not adduced in evidence, might have played its part in her verdict. The moment when she disclosed any of that information to her fellow jurors she further prejudiced the administration of justice. In the result, the jury was rightly discharged from returning a verdict and a new trial was ordered. The unfortunate complainant had to give evidence of his ordeal on a second occasion. The time of the other members of the jury was wasted, and the public was put to additional unnecessary expense. The damage to the administration of justice is obvious.' (Lord Chief Justice, para 28)

    e. *AG v Davey* and *AG v Beard* [2013] EWHC 2317

(Admin), [2013] All ER (D) 391 — a juror researched a defendant on the Internet while serving, the second posted information about the case on Twitter; in a combined decision the jours were found in contempt of court

    f. Research has shown that jours are not always clear on what is permitted and what is not; most are unaware that jours can be prosecuted for misconduct

    g. Law Commission Review, 2013 — recommended the new statutory criminal offense for a sworn juror who researches information related to the case in which they are serving

  ii. Strengthening the laws

    a. Criminal Justice and Courts Act 2015

      - s.71 — offense for a juror to intentionally research information during the trial period, where he knows or reasonably knows that the information maybe or is relevant to the case

      - s.72 — offense for one juror to pass to another juror information found by research not presented in court

      - s.73 — offense for unsure in a case before a court to purposefully engage in prohibited conduct during the trial.

      - s.74 — offense to intentionally disclose information about jury deliberations, or to solicit such information

8.4. Non-jury trials

  i. s. 44 Criminal Justice Act 2003

    a. Allows trials to be heard and decided by a judge alone in special circumstances

      - A jury would be a disadvantage (i.e., in danger of jury tampering, or where it has taken place)

    b. Jury tampering refers two situations where a juror maybe bribed, Intimidated, or interfere with in some other way

    c. This was done in northern Ireland in the 1970s because of the ongoing civil conflicts and instances of jury intimidation ("Diplock Courts")

  ii. To grant a nonjury trial, the court must be satisfied that

    a. there is evidence that jury tampering could take place

    b. the danger is significant enough that is in the interests of justice to proceed without a trial

  iii. The first use of this provision was in February 2010, dealing with a violent armed robbery at Heathrow airport in 2004;

the police found that two members of the jury had been approached with intent to tamper

iv. *J, S, M v R* [2010] EWCA Crim 1755 — non-jury trials are only permitted in extreme cases, i.e., where police protection of jurors would be unreasonable and intrusive

    a. 'The trial of a serious criminal offence without a jury ... remains and must remain the decision of last resort, only to be ordered when the court is sure (not that it entertains doubts, suspicions or reservations) that the statutory conditions are fulfilled.' (Lord Chief Justice)

v. *KS v R* [2010] EWCA Crim 1756 — an Nonjury trial application was rejected because I'm Only limited protection of a juror was necessary in proportion to the threat.

8.5. Conclusion

i. The courts take hey careful View of proceeding with non-jury trials in the Crown Court

ii. This reflects the common law view of the importance of the role of citizens in the judicial system

iii. The right to trial by jury is considered an important right in democratic societies and part of the rule of law

iv. Studies have shown the public has high confidence in jury trials

9. Appeals

9.1. Introduction

i. An important part of the rule of law and fairness of the justice system is the ease with which a criminal case can be appealed

    a. It can correct mistakes to avoid injustice

    b. It reinforces due process concepts

    c. Remedies unfair or incorrect decisions

    d. Ensures consistency in the system allowing for development of clear legal rules in precedent

ii. Either the defense or the prosecution can appeal against conviction and sentence

iii. Magistrate court cases are appeals to the Crown Court

iv. Crown court cases are appealed to the court of appeal, and a further appeal to the Supreme Court

v. If all appeals are exhausted, but one party insists that justice has not been done this is referred to as a miscarriage of justice

    a. Allegation that innocent person has been convicted, or a guilty person has been acquitted

    b. There are procedures for special cases to review such miscarriages

9.2. Prosecution appeals

    i. s.36 Criminal Justice Act 1972 — the attorney general can make a reference on a point of law that is unclear or doubtful; has no affect on the acquitted defendant regardless of the decision

    ii. s.36 Criminal Justice Act 1988 — prosecution cannot appeal a sentence, but they can appeal if they think the sentence is too lenient; the Court of Appeal can increase it if justified

    iii. s.75–76 Criminal Justice Act 2003 — inside of circumstances, a retrial can be ordered despite an acquittal; requires new and compelling evidence of guilt and that the public interest requires it

9.3. Defense appeals

    i. On appeal from the magistrates Court, the Crown Court holds a complete rehearing

    ii. And appeal from the Crown Court goes to the Court of Appeal (criminal division)

    iii. Criminal Appeal Act 1968 — the defendant who wishes to appeal against conviction or sentence must obtain permission from the Court of Appeal

    iv. Further appeal can be made to the Supreme Court, but only if the Court of Appeal certifies that there is a Point of law of public importance which should be considered by the Supreme Court; either the Court of Appeal or the Supreme Court can't approve of the appeal

    v. For the Court of Appeal to allow and appeal against conviction, it must believe that the conviction is unsafe otherwise the appeal is to be dismissed

9.4. Criminal Cases Review Commission

    i. Before April 1977 the homes secretary reviewed applications of miscarriages of justice

        a. Referred cases back to the Court of Appeal when determined to be valid

    ii. Royal Commission on Criminal Justice Report (1993)

        a. Stated that it was incompatible with separation of powers principle for the home secretary to review allegations of miscarriages of justice (as an elected official in the executive, the home secretary was responsible for law and order in the police, and should not be making such

decisions)
- b. Recommended the formation of an independent Office to
  - Evaluate miscarriages of justice
  - Arrange for investigation if needed
  - Refer appropriate cases to the Court of Appeal

iii. Criminal Appeal Act 1995 — established the Criminal Cases Review Commission
- a. To refer cases for reconsideration when it found A 'Real possibility' let the conviction, verdict, finding, or sentence would not be upheld (the commission found evidence that was not presented at trial)
- b. Once a case has been referred back, the CCRC has no other role
- c. May investigate cases on its own volition, or those who have been referred to it by individual
- d. Made up of publicly appointed commissioners, with managers, advisers for legal and investigatory work, casework, and administrative staff
- e. 2011/12 the CCRC received over 1000 applications and referred about 3.5%; 50 to 70% of those are allowed by the court

iv. The Innocence Network UK report (Feb 2013)
- a. Questioned only one option for convicted persons to appeal miscarriages of justice (through the CCRC)
- b. Argued that the 'Real possibility' test favored the Court of Appeal, preventing a possibly genuine wrongful conviction if the court filed the case lacks legal merit
- c. Recommended that the 'Real possibility' test be replaced with one that would allow the CCRC more independence and its review and consideration

v. House of Commons Justice Committee Report (Mar 2015)
- a. Examined whether the CCRC what's fulfilling its mandate
- b. Whether the statutory powers and resources of the CCRC were sufficient for its mandate and to promote confidence in the system
- c. Concluded that the CCRC was fulfilling its mandate, but more should be done to promote its work; it should be given the resources and powers it needs to perform properly.

COURSE DIAGRAMS

Introduction

These diagrams offer a visual aid to all the topics and subtopics in the same order as the Course Outlines, including the key terms, cases, and statutes.

Suggested study plan:

1. Look over the chapter which corresponds to the chapter you are studying.
2. Read the your assigned readings and do any assigned activities.
3. Review the Course Outline for the current subject, then the VisuaLaw Diagrams. See if you can discuss each item in detail just by looking at the Diagrams. Go back over the reading material to strengthen the areas in which you are weak.
4. Come back and repeat this periodically for each chapter throughout the course.

When you are preparing for your exams, use the VisuaLaw Diagrams as an aid to memorization and to test yourself on the topics. Test yourself by recreating the diagrams from memory until. Pretend you are teaching the topic to someone else.

1. INTRODUCTION

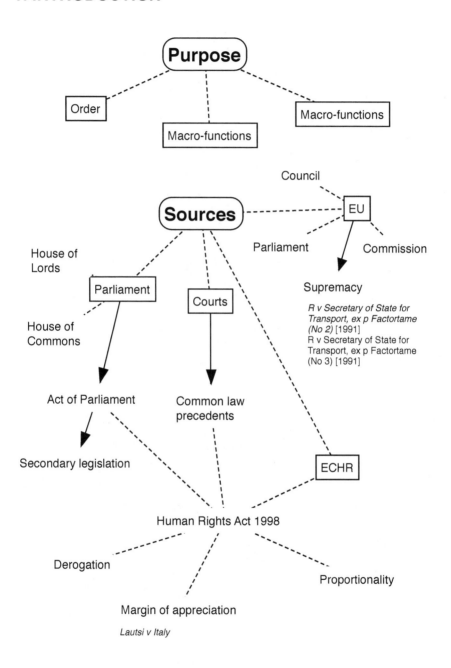

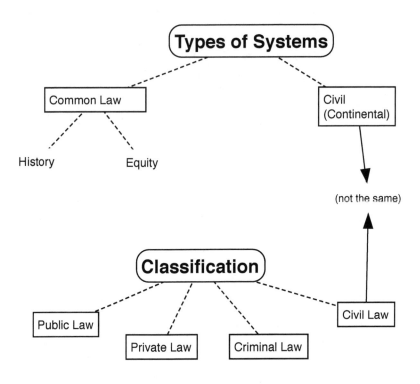

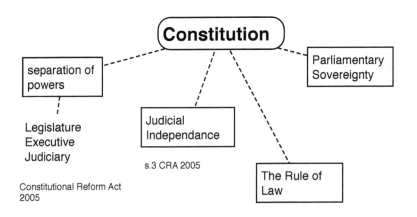

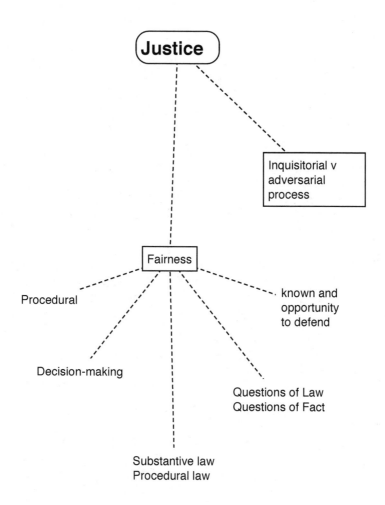

2. COURTS

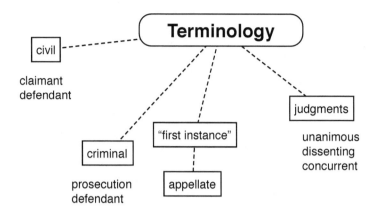

Terminology

civil
- claimant
- defendant

criminal
- prosecution
- defendant

"first instance"
- appellate

judgments
- unanimous
- dissenting
- concurrent

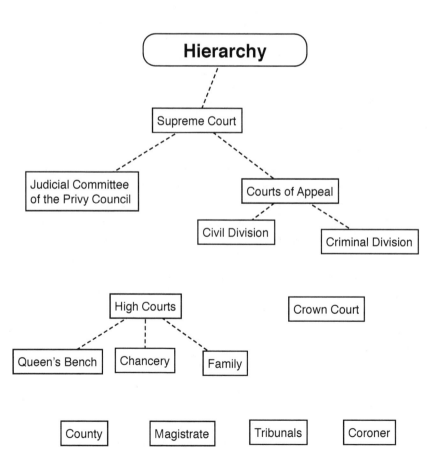

Hierarchy

Supreme Court

Judicial Committee of the Privy Council

Courts of Appeal
- Civil Division
- Criminal Division

High Courts
- Queen's Bench
- Chancery
- Family

Crown Court

County

Magistrate

Tribunals

Coroner

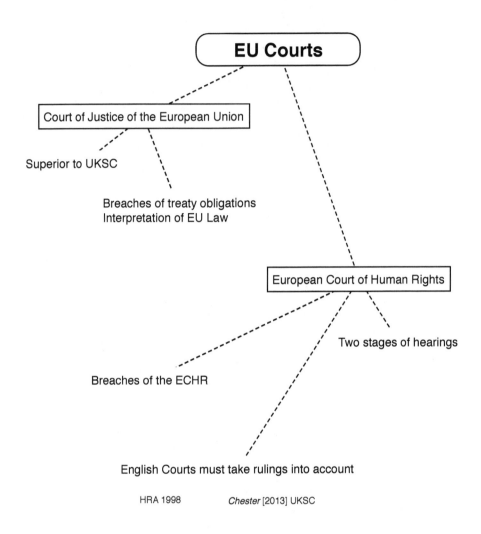

3. PRECEDENT

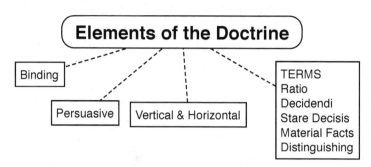

Elements of the Doctrine

Binding

Persuasive

Vertical & Horizontal

TERMS
Ratio
Decidendi
Stare Decisis
Material Facts
Distinguishing

The Practice Statement (Judicial Precedent) [1966]

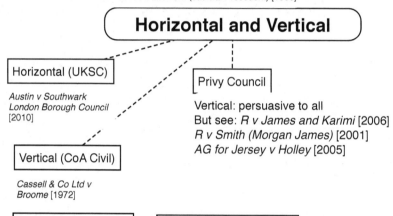

Horizontal and Vertical

Horizontal (UKSC)

Austin v Southwark London Borough Council [2010]

Privy Council

Vertical: persuasive to all
But see: *R v James and Karimi* [2006]
R v Smith (Morgan James) [2001]
AG for Jersey v Holley [2005]

Vertical (CoA Civil)

Cassell & Co Ltd v Broome [1972]

Horizontal (CoA Civil)

Young v Bristol Aeroplane Co Ltd [1944]

implied overruling

per incuriam decisions
Morelle v Wakeling [1955]

Horizontal (CoA Criminal)

R v Taylor [1950]

Young v Bristol Aeroplane

Divisional Courts of High Court

Vertical: UKSC, CoA
Horizontal: own decisions
Young v Bristol Aeroplane

High Court

Vertical: UKSC, CoA, Div Courts
Horizontal: own decisions persuasive

Crown Court

Vertical: All above, bind all below
Horizontal: own decisions

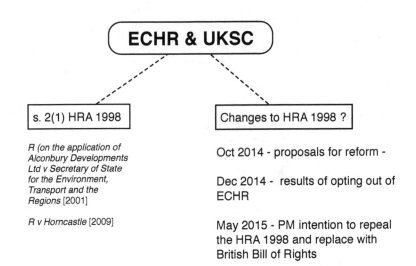

ECHR & UKSC

s. 2(1) HRA 1998

R (on the application of Alconbury Developments Ltd v Secretary of State for the Environment, Transport and the Regions [2001]

R v Horncastle [2009]

Changes to HRA 1998 ?

Oct 2014 - proposals for reform -

Dec 2014 - results of opting out of ECHR

May 2015 - PM intention to repeal the HRA 1998 and replace with British Bill of Rights

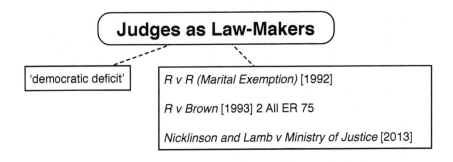

Judges as Law-Makers

'democratic deficit'

R v R (Marital Exemption) [1992]

R v Brown [1993] 2 All ER 75

Nicklinson and Lamb v Ministry of Justice [2013]

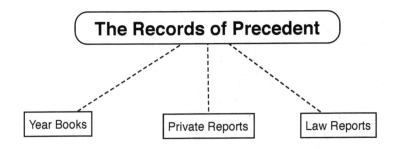

The Records of Precedent

Year Books

Private Reports

Law Reports

4. STATUTORY INTERPRETATION

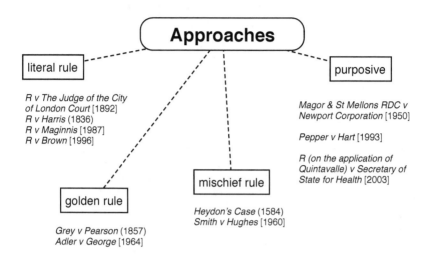

Approaches

literal rule

R v The Judge of the City of London Court [1892]
R v Harris (1836)
R v Maginnis [1987]
R v Brown [1996]

purposive

Magor & St Mellons RDC v Newport Corporation [1950]

Pepper v Hart [1993]

R (on the application of Quintavalle) v Secretary of State for Health [2003]

golden rule

Grey v Pearson (1857)
Adler v George [1964]

mischief rule

Heydon's Case (1584)
Smith v Hughes [1960]

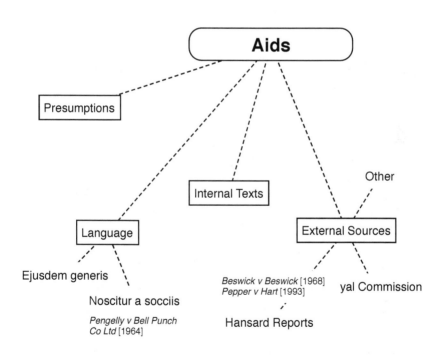

Aids

Presumptions

Internal Texts

Other

Language

External Sources

Ejusdem generis

Noscitur a socciis

Pengelly v Bell Punch Co Ltd [1964]

Beswick v Beswick [1968]
Pepper v Hart [1993]

yal Commission

Hansard Reports

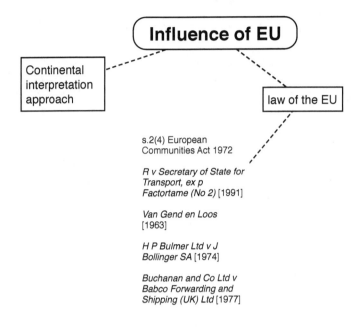

Influence of EU

Continental interpretation approach

law of the EU

s.2(4) European Communities Act 1972

R v Secretary of State for Transport, ex p Factortame (No 2) [1991]

Van Gend en Loos [1963]

H P Bulmer Ltd v J Bollinger SA [1974]

Buchanan and Co Ltd v Babco Forwarding and Shipping (UK) Ltd [1977]

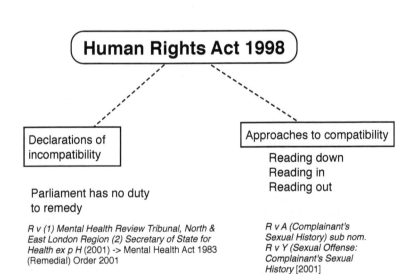

Human Rights Act 1998

Declarations of incompatibility

Approaches to compatibility

Reading down
Reading in
Reading out

Parliament has no duty to remedy

R v (1) Mental Health Review Tribunal, North & East London Region (2) Secretary of State for Health ex p H (2001) -> Mental Health Act 1983 (Remedial) Order 2001

Bellinger v Bellinger [2003] -> Gender Recognition Act 2004.

A v Secretary of State for the Home Department [2004] -> Prevention of Terrorism Act 2005

R v A (Complainant's Sexual History) sub nom. R v Y (Sexual Offense: Complainant's Sexual History [2001]

Ghaidan v Godlin-Mendoza [2004]

5. JUDICIARY

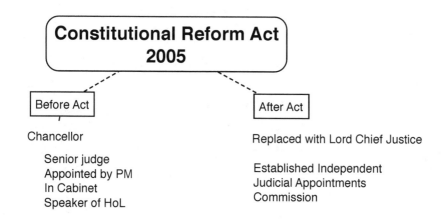

Constitutional Reform Act 2005

Before Act

Chancellor

Senior judge
Appointed by PM
In Cabinet
Speaker of HoL

After Act

Replaced with Lord Chief Justice

Established Independent
Judicial Appointments
Commission

McGonnell v UK [2000]

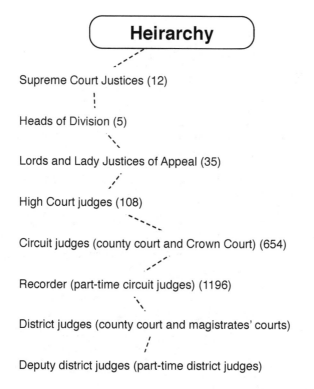

Heirarchy

Supreme Court Justices (12)

Heads of Division (5)

Lords and Lady Justices of Appeal (35)

High Court judges (108)

Circuit judges (county court and Crown Court) (654)

Recorder (part-time circuit judges) (1196)

District judges (county court and magistrates' courts)

Deputy district judges (part-time district judges)

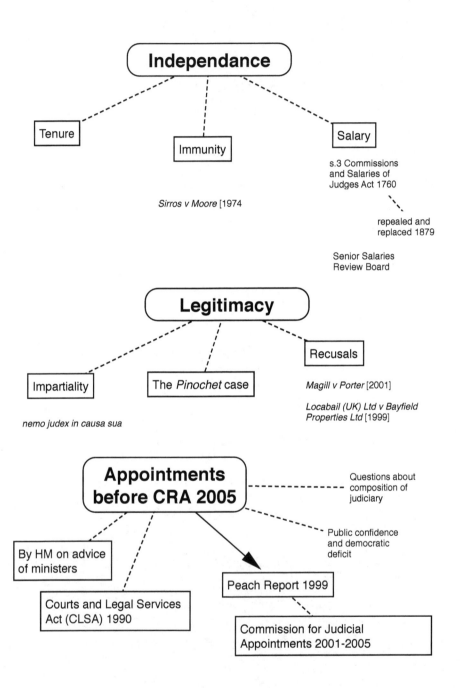

Independance

Tenure

Immunity

Sirros v Moore [1974

Salary

s.3 Commissions
and Salaries of
Judges Act 1760

repealed and
replaced 1879

Senior Salaries
Review Board

Legitimacy

Impartiality

nemo judex in causa sua

The *Pinochet* case

Recusals

Magill v Porter [2001]

*Locabail (UK) Ltd v Bayfield
Properties Ltd* [1999]

**Appointments
before CRA 2005**

Questions about
composition of
judiciary

By HM on advice
of ministers

Public confidence
and democratic
deficit

Courts and Legal Services
Act (CLSA) 1990

Peach Report 1999

Commission for Judicial
Appointments 2001-2005

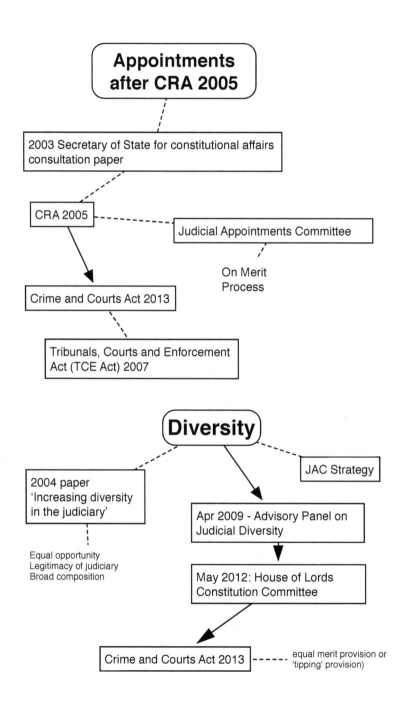

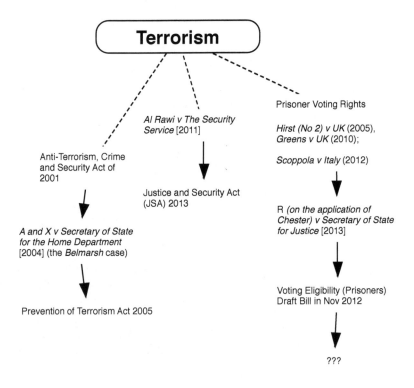

Judicial Power and Constitutionality

Vernon Bogdanor, 2006 ⟶ Democracy to 'juristocracy' ?

Re A (Children) [2000]

Human Rights

Terrorism

Anti-Terrorism, Crime
and Security Act of
2001

*A and X v Secretary of State
for the Home Department*
[2004] (the *Belmarsh* case)

Prevention of Terrorism Act 2005

*Al Rawi v The Security
Service* [2011]

Justice and Security Act
(JSA) 2013

Prisoner Voting Rights

Hirst (No 2) v UK (2005),
Greens v UK (2010);

Scoppola v Italy (2012)

R *(on the application of
Chester) v Secretary of State
for Justice* [2013]

Voting Eligibility (Prisoners)
Draft Bill in Nov 2012

???

6. CIVIL JUSTICE SYSTEM

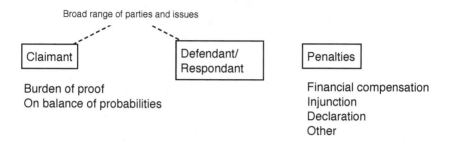

Broad range of parties and issues

Claimant	Defendant/ Respondant	Penalties

Burden of proof
On balance of probabilities

Financial compensation
Injunction
Declaration
Other

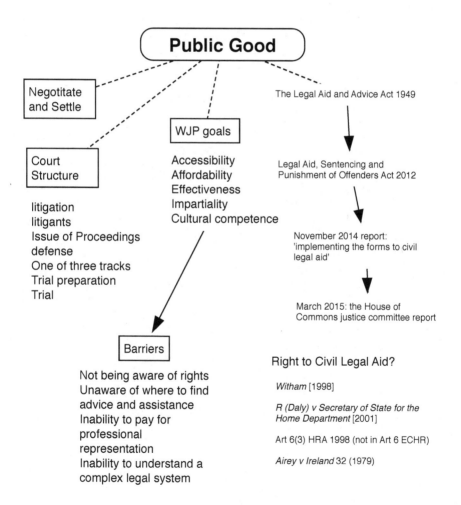

Public Good

Negotitate and Settle

The Legal Aid and Advice Act 1949

WJP goals

Court Structure

Accessibility
Affordability
Effectiveness
Impartiality
Cultural competence

litigation
litigants
Issue of Proceedings
defense
One of three tracks
Trial preparation
Trial

Legal Aid, Sentencing and
Punishment of Offenders Act 2012

November 2014 report:
'implementing the forms to civil
legal aid'

March 2015: the House of
Commons justice committee report

Barriers

Not being aware of rights
Unaware of where to find
advice and assistance
Inability to pay for
professional
representation
Inability to understand a
complex legal system

Right to Civil Legal Aid?

Witham [1998]

*R (Daly) v Secretary of State for the
Home Department* [2001]

Art 6(3) HRA 1998 (not in Art 6 ECHR)

Airey v Ireland 32 (1979)

Accessibility

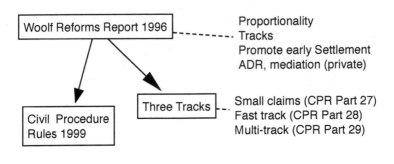

Woolf Reforms Report 1996

- Proportionality
- Tracks
- Promote early Settlement
- ADR, mediation (private)

Civil Procedure Rules 1999

Three Tracks

- Small claims (CPR Part 27)
- Fast track (CPR Part 28)
- Multi-track (CPR Part 29)

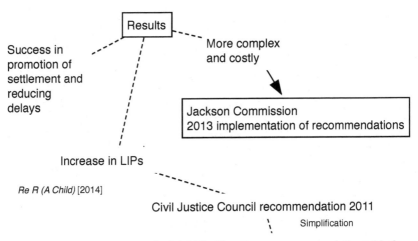

Results

Success in promotion of settlement and reducing delays

More complex and costly

Jackson Commission
2013 implementation of recommendations

Increase in LIPs

Re R (A Child) [2014]

Civil Justice Council recommendation 2011

Simplification

Judicial Working Group recommendations 2013

More inquisitorial approach, flexibility

Mole v Hunter [2014]
Re C (A Child) [2013]
Re W (A Child) [2013]
Re D (A Child) [2014]

National Audit Office, *report on implementation of legal aid reforms*, Nov 2014

Civil Justice Council Report, Dec 2014

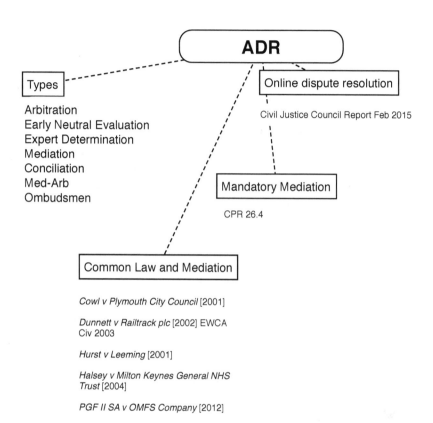

ADR

Types

Arbitration
Early Neutral Evaluation
Expert Determination
Mediation
Conciliation
Med-Arb
Ombudsmen

Online dispute resolution

Civil Justice Council Report Feb 2015

Mandatory Mediation

CPR 26.4

Common Law and Mediation

Cowl v Plymouth City Council [2001]

Dunnett v Railtrack plc [2002] EWCA Civ 2003

Hurst v Leeming [2001]

Halsey v Milton Keynes General NHS Trust [2004]

PGF II SA v OMFS Company [2012]

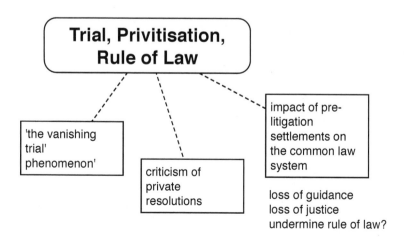

Trial, Privitisation, Rule of Law

'the vanishing trial' phenomenon'

criticism of private resolutions

impact of pre-litigation settlements on the common law system

loss of guidance
loss of justice
undermine rule of law?

7. CRIMINAL JUSTICE SYSTEM

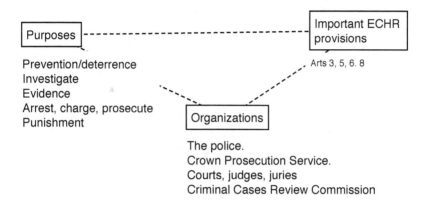

Purposes

Prevention/deterrence
Investigate
Evidence
Arrest, charge, prosecute
Punishment

Important ECHR provisions

Arts 3, 5, 6. 8

Organizations

The police.
Crown Prosecution Service.
Courts, judges, juries
Criminal Cases Review Commission

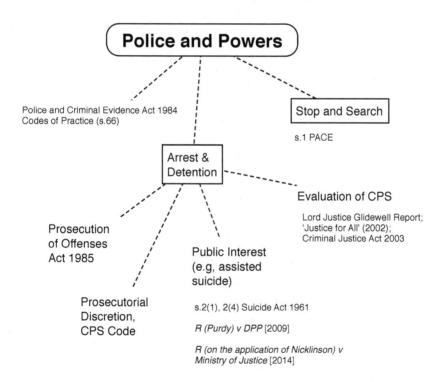

Police and Powers

Police and Criminal Evidence Act 1984
Codes of Practice (s.66)

Stop and Search

s.1 PACE

Arrest & Detention

Evaluation of CPS

Lord Justice Glidewell Report;
'Justice for All' (2002);
Criminal Justice Act 2003

Prosecution
of Offenses
Act 1985

Public Interest
(e.g, assisted
suicide)

Prosecutorial
Discretion,
CPS Code

s.2(1), 2(4) Suicide Act 1961

R (Purdy) v DPP [2009]

*R (on the application of Nicklinson) v
Ministry of Justice* [2014]

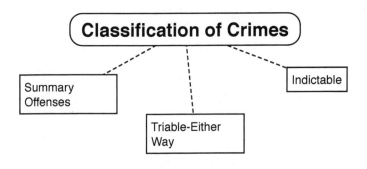

Classification of Crimes

Summary Offenses

Triable-Either Way

Indictable

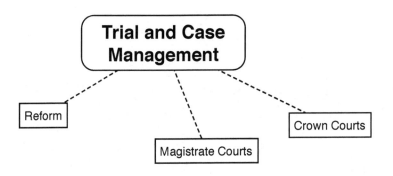

Trial and Case Management

Reform

Magistrate Courts

Crown Courts

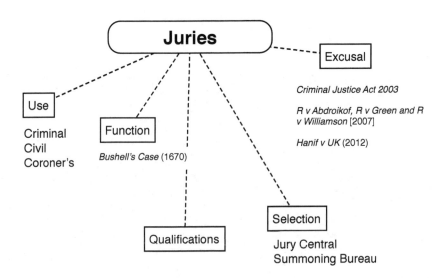

Juries

Excusal

Use

Criminal
Civil
Coroner's

Function

Bushell's Case (1670)

Qualifications

Selection

Jury Central
Summoning Bureau

Criminal Justice Act 2003

R v Abdroikof, R v Green and R v Williamson [2007]

Hanif v UK (2012)

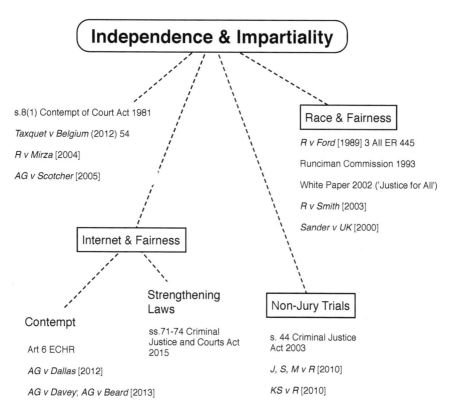

Independence & Impartiality

s.8(1) Contempt of Court Act 1981

Taxquet v Belgium (2012) 54

R v Mirza [2004]

AG v Scotcher [2005]

Race & Fairness

R v Ford [1989] 3 All ER 445

Runciman Commission 1993

White Paper 2002 ('Justice for All')

R v Smith [2003]

Sander v UK [2000]

Internet & Fairness

Strengthening Laws

ss.71-74 Criminal Justice and Courts Act 2015

Non-Jury Trials

s. 44 Criminal Justice Act 2003

J, S, M v R [2010]

KS v R [2010]

Contempt

Art 6 ECHR

AG v Dallas [2012]

AG v Davey; AG v Beard [2013]

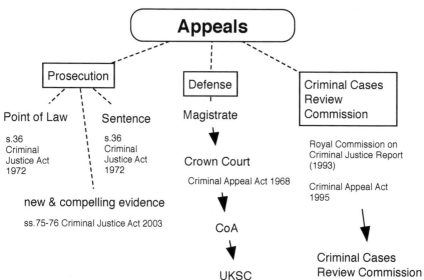

Appeals

Prosecution

Point of Law

s.36 Criminal Justice Act 1972

Sentence

s.36 Criminal Justice Act 1972

new & compelling evidence

ss.75-76 Criminal Justice Act 2003

Defense

Magistrate

↓

Crown Court

Criminal Appeal Act 1968

↓

CoA

↓

UKSC

Criminal Cases Review Commission

Royal Commission on Criminal Justice Report (1993)

Criminal Appeal Act 1995

↓

Criminal Cases Review Commission

EXAM STUDY SHEETS

Exam Study Sheets are condensed outlines, based on the Course Outlines above. These are designed to help you get the "big picture" for revising and for testing yourself in preparation for exams. Each Exam Sheet contains 1–5 pages on each of the topics covered in the Course Outlines and Diagrams, including a few key statutes and cases for each.

Suggested study plan.

1. Look over the readings, Course Outlines, and Course Diagrams for the first topic.

2. Using the Exam Study Sheet for the first topic, test yourself on each item. Can you explain each one in detail? Can you remember important elements, discuss cases and statutes, and explain the concepts?

3. Review the Course outlines and Diagrams in areas where you are weak. Refer to your course materials to revise and review.

4. Repeat for each topic in the course.

When you are preparing for your exams, use the Exam Study Sheet as one of your tools for testing yourself.

1. Introduction

1. Purpose of Law
    1.1. Order
    1.2. Partington: Macrofunctions
    1.3. Partington: Micro functions

2. Sources of Law
    2.1. Parliament
        i. Two Chambers
        ii. Act of Parliament
        iii. Process
        iv. Precedence over?
        v. Primary legislation
        vi. Secondary legislation
    2.2. Courts
        i. Common law in contrast to statutes
        ii. Developed over many years, to origins of English common law in the 12th century
        iii. Precedence
    2.3. EU
        i. An economic and political agreement based on treaties
        ii. The rule of law
        iii. All members of the EU are required to keep the laws of the EU (UK joined in 1973)
            a. European Parliament, European Council, European Commission
            b. Supremacy of EU law case
                - *R v Secretary of State for Transport, ex p Factortame (No 2)* [1991] 1 All ER 70, HL/ ECJ and R v Secretary of State for Transport, ex p Factortame (No 3) [1991] 3 All ER 769, ECJ
    2.4. The European Convention on Human Rights (ECHR)
        i. An international treaty
        ii. Human Rights Act 1998
            a. Right to life (Art 2)
            b. Prohibition of Torture (Art 4)
            c. Prohibition of slavery and forced labour (art 5)
            d. Right to liberty and security (Art 5)
            e. Right to a fair trial (Art 6)

      f. No punishment without law (Art 7)

      g. Right to respect of family and private life (Art 8)

      h. Freedom of thought, conscience, and religion (Art 9)

      i. Freedom of expression (Art 10)

      j. Freedom of assembly and association (Art 11)

      k. Prohibition of discrimination (Art 14)

      l. Right not to be subjected to the death penalty (Arts 1, 2 of Protocol 6)

      m. Right to free elections (Art 3 of Protocol 1)

   iii. Derogation

      a. Some of these rights are absolute and inalienable

      b. Some are contingent

   iv. 'Margin of Appreciation'

      a. *Lautsi v Italy* (Application no. 30814/06)

   v. Proportionality

      a. *de Freitas v Permanent Secretary of Ministry of Agriculture, Fisheries, Lands and Housing* [1999] 1 AC 69

3. Types of Legal Systems

  3.1. Civil Law (Continental) Systems

  3.2. Common Law Systems

   i. Roots

   ii. Features

   iii. History of Common Law

      a. Norman conquest in 1066,

      b. Kings court (*Curia Regis*)

      c. Henry II in 1154

      d. Practice of using precedents

   d. Common law's contributions to social order

   e. Equity

      a. creation of the Court of Chancery

      b. By the 19th century the Court of Chancery had become expensive and cases were lengthy

      c. In 1873, the courts of equity were combined with the common law courts (Judicature Act 1873-1875)

4. Legal Classification

  4.1. Meaning of the term 'Common Law'

   i. In contrast to Statute Law

   ii. In contrast to Equity

   iii. In contrast to Civil Law

  4.2. Public law

i. The relationship between citizens and their state

ii. Judicial review is the process where citizens can challenge decisions of the state

iii. *R v Lord Chancellor ex p Witham* [1997] 2 All ER 779

4.3. Private law

i. relationships between individuals

4.4. Criminal law

4.5. Civil law

5. Constitution and the Legal System

5.1. Principles

i. Separation of powers

    a. The legislature

    b. The executive

    c. The judiciary

    d. Constitutional Reform Act 2005

ii. Judicial independance

    a. s3 CRA 2005

iii. Parliamentary Sovereignty

iv. The Rule of Law

    a. Lord Bingham's eight ingredients of the rule of law

    b. Judicial independence and the rule of law

      - Bangalore Principles of Judicial Conduct (2002):

    c. Four universal principles

    d. Factors that should be evident:

6. Justice

6.1. Fair justice and fair process

i. Procedural fairness

ii. Fairness in decision-making

iii. The laws should be known and the accused have an opportunity to defend themselves

iv. Law and facts

    a. "questions of fact"

    b. "questions of law"

v. Substantive and procedural law

    a. Substantive law

    b. Procedural law

6.2. Inquisitorial and adversarial procedure

i. Common law court procedures, As opposed to civil law court procedures, are adversarial

ii. Civil law jurisdictions engage in a more inquisitorial procedure

2. The Courts

1. Distinctions
    1.1. Civil Courts
        i. Purpose
        ii. The claimant
        iii. The defendant
    1.2. Criminal courts
        i. Purpose
        ii. The prosecution
        iii. The defendant
    1.3. Courts of First Instance and Appellate Coiurts
        i. Appeal court
        ii. First instance
    1.4. Judgements
        i. A Unanimous judgment
        ii. A dissenting judgment
        iii. A concurrent judgment

2. Hierarchy
    2.1. The United Kingdom Supreme Court
        i. Constitutional Reform Act 2005 Part 3
        ii. Highest court of appeal in the UK (except criminal cases from Scotland)
        iii. Supposed to apply the EU laws that are relevant
        iv. Can ask EU courts for opinions and help
    2.2. Judicial Committee of the Privy Council
    2.3. Courts of Appeal
        i. Court of Appeal Civil Division
            a. Mostly deal with appeals from first instance cases in the High Court and County courts
        ii. Court of Appeal Criminal Division
            a. The court hears appeals against conviction or sentence from the Crown Court, And issues guidances for the lower courts
    2.4. High Courts (hears criminal and civil cases at first instance and on appeal)
        i. Queen's Bench
            a. Hears cases in tort, contract, admiralty, commercial

      disputes, Technology and construction disputes, and
      includes an administrative court for judicial review
   ii. Chancery
     a. Hear cases concerning bankruptcy, ownership of land,
       trusts and just speeded wills, patents
   iii. Family
     a. Hear cases involving matrimony, adoption and other
       children's issues
2.5. Crown Court
   i. Both appellate and first instance
   ii. Mostly serious criminal offenses
   iii. Appeals from magistrates Court
   iv. Criminal cases usually have a jury
2.6. Family Court
   i. Crime and Courts Act 2013; The Family Procedure
     (Amendment No) Rules 2013/3204
   ii. Deals with family cases that previously would have been
     heard by the High Court, County courts, and magistrate court
2.7. County Courts
   i. civil law: contract, tort, insolvency, probate, etc.
2.8. Magistrate Courts
   i. Almost all criminal cases (preliminary before being sent to
     High Court), range of civil cases
2.9. Tribunals
   i. Does not administer any part of the judicial power of the state
     (*A-G v British Broadcasting Corporation*, 3 All ER 61 (1980).
   ii. Specialist bodies dealing with specialist law
2.10. Coroners
   i. Matters of sudden deaths
   ii. Inquisitorial process

3. European Courts
3.1. Court of Justice of the European Union (CJEU
   i. This court is superior to the UK Supreme Court in disputes
     about European law
   ii. Hears cases about breaches of obligations under European
     treaties, interpretation of European law
3.2. European Court of Human Rights (ECtHR)
   i. Breaches of the ECHR
   ii. The first stage
   iii. The second stage
   iv. No authority over the English courts, but the HRA 1998 must

be taken into consideration (the Supreme Court usually follows the decisions of this court)
a. *Chester* [2013] UKSC 63.

3. Precedent

1. **Introduction**
    1.1. Doctrine of Judicial Precedent
        i. Binding precedent
        ii. stare decisis
        iii. Binding and persuasive precedent
            a. *Ratio* of the Privy Council
            b. *Ratio* of superior courts in other jurisdictions of the common-law
            c. High court judges referring to decisions by other High Court judges
        iv. Vertical and horizontal
            a. Vertical precedent
            b. Horizontal precedent
        v. *ratio decidendi* and *obiter dicta*
    1.2. Material facts
    1.3. Distinguishing
    1.4. Loss of binding authority
2. **The courts and precedent**
    2.1. The Judge-Made Doctrine
    2.2. Do Judges Make Law or Declare What It Is?
        i. William Blackstone
        ii. *Midland Silicone Ltd v Scruttons Ltd* [1962] AC 446.
        iii. Lord Reid, *The Judge as Law Maker*
        iv. *National Westminster Bank v Spectrum Plus* [2005] 2 AC 680
3. **In practice**
    3.1. Vertical and Horizontal Precedent
        i. Horizontal
            a. *London Street Tramways Ltd v London County Council* [1898] AC 375
        ii. The Practice Statement (Judicial Precedent) [1966] 3 All ER 77
        iii. Horizontal in the UKSC
            a. *Austin v Southwark London Borough Council* [2010] UKSC 28, [2010] 4 All ER 16
    3.2. Vertical in the CoA (Civil Division)

     i. *Cassell & Co Ltd v Broome* [1972] AC 1027

3.3. Horizontal in the CoA (Civil Division)

     i. *Young v Bristol Aeroplane Co Ltd* [1944] 2 All ER 293

     ii. implied overruling

     iii. per incuriam decisions

        a. *Morelle v Wakeling* [1955] 2 QB 379, 406

     iv. Court of Appeal decision is in conflict with it earlier decision
of the Supreme Court.

        a. *Miliangos v George Frank (Textiles) Ltd* [1976] AC 443
and *Schorsch Meier GmbH v Hennin* [1975] QB 416 and
Havanah, 1960.

     v. Should CoA be able to depart from its own earlier decision?

        a. Settled in *Davis v Johnson* [1978] 1 All ER 841 (CA),
[1978] 1 All ER 1132 (HL).

3.4. Horizontal in the CoA (Criminal Division)

     i. *R v Taylor* [1950] 2 All ER 170; *Young v Bristol Aeroplane*

3.5. Divisional Courts of the High Court

     i. Vertical - divisional courts of the High Court are bound by
House of Lords, Supreme Court, Court of Appeal; decisions of
the divisional courts are binding on courts below it

     ii. Horizontal - divisional courts are bound by their own
decisions, but *Young v Bristol Aeroplane* can be applied

     iii. High Court - bound by the House of Lords, Supreme Court,
court of Appeal, divisional courts. The high courts own
decisions are highly persuasive, but not bound by them

     iv. Crown Court - bound by all courts above it, By its own
decisions, and bind all courts below it

     v. Privy Council

        a. Privy Council decisions do not bind other courts, but are
persuasive

        b. But see *R v James and Karimi* [2006] EWCA Crim 14; *R
v Smith (Morgan James)* [2001] 1 AC 146; *AG for Jersey
v Holley* [2005] UKPC 23;

4. The ECHR and the UKSC

4.1. s. 2(1) HRA 1998: UK court must "take into account"

     i. *R (on the application of Alconbury Developments Ltd v
Secretary of State for the Environment, Transport and the
Regions* [2001] UKHL 23

     ii. *R v Horncastle* [2009] UKSC 14

4.2. Changes to the HRA 1998?

     i. Oct 2014 - proposals for reform -

  ii. Dec 2014 - results of opting out of ECHR

  iii. May 2015 - PM Cameron announced intention to repeal the HRA 1998 and replaced with a British Bill of Rights.

5. Judges as law-makers

 5.1. 'democratic deficit.'

 5.2. *R v R (Marital Exemption)* [1992] 1 AC 599; *R v Brown* [1993] 2 All ER 75; *Nicklinson and Lamb v Ministry of Justice* [2013] EWCA Civ 961

6. The history of law-making

 6.1. Year Books

 6.2. Private Reports

 6.3. Law Reports

4. Statutory Interpretation

1. **Introduction**
   1.1. Definition
   1.2. Guidelines: *Sussex Peerage Claim* (1844),
2. **The Difficulty**
   2.1. features of statutes that make interpretation difficult
      i. Ellipsis
      ii. Broad terms
      iii. Unforeseeable developments due to social or economic changes
      iv. Errors in printing or drafting
3. **Reasons for Interpretation**
   3.1. Judge must determine the meaning, scope, and applicability of a statute to a given context
4. **Approaches**
   4.1. Literal Rule (Literalism)
      i. Apply the ordinary meaning of words
      ii. *R v The Judge of the City of London Court* [1892] 1 QB 273
      iii. *R v Harris* (1836) 7 Car & P 446, 173 ER 198
      iv. *R v Maginnis* [1987] 1 All ER 907 (HL) interpreting s.5(3) Misuse of Drugs Act 1971
      v. *R v Brown* [1996] 1 All ER 545 (HL) interpreting s.5(2)(b) of the Data Protection Act 1984
   4.2. Golden Rule
      i. Uses the literary approach, but if this results in an 'absurd' result, the words can be modified
      ii. *Grey v Pearson* (1857) 6 HL Cas 106
      iii. *Adler v George* [1964] 2 QB 7 interpreting s.3 of the Official Secrets Act 1920
   4.3. Mischief Rule
      i. *Heydon's Case* (1584) 3 Co Rep 7a, 76 ER 637
      ii. Review the state of the common law before the Act was passed
      iii. Determine the wrongdoing the Act was intended to address
      iv. Interpret the law in light of that intended purpose (this is similar to the purpose rule below)
      v. *Smith v Hughes* [1960] 2 All ER 859, interpreting s.1 Street Offences Act 1959
   4.4. Purposive

      i. Takes a wider view by deciding what Parliament intended to achieve by writing and passing the law—'the spirit of the Act'

      ii. *Magor & St Mellons RDC v Newport Corporation* [1950] 2 All ER 1226 (CA); [1952] AC 189 (HL),

      iii. *Pepper v Hart* [1993] 1 All ER 42; *R (on the application of Quintavalle) v Secretary of State for Health* [2003] 2 AC 687

  4.5. Giving Effect to the Intention of Parliament

5. Aids

  5.1. Presumptions

      i. Not retrospective (esp in criminal law)

        a. Exception: s.58(8) of the Criminal Justice Act 2003 - allows prosecution to appeal against acquittal

      ii. Changes to basic rules must be clearly defined

        a. *Leach v R* [1912] AC 305

  5.2. Langauge

      i. Ejusdem generis

        a. general words that follow specific words should be read in light of the preceding specific words

        b. Sunday Observance Act 1677

      ii. Noscitur a socciis

        a. Words should be given the meaning that derives from the immediate context

        b. *Pengelly v Bell Punch Co Ltd* [1964] 2 All ER 945 interpreting s.28 of the Factories Act 1961

  5.3. Internal texts

  5.4. External sources

      i. Hansard Reports

        a. *Beswick v Beswick* [1968] AC 58; *Pepper v Hart* [1993] 1 All ER 42

      ii. Royal Commission, etc.

      iii. Other

        a. International treaties, other Acts, dictionaries, etc.

6. Influence of he EU

  6.1. Continental Interpretation

      i. Substantive law is found in written codes using general language,

      ii. Judges interpret codes to apply to each situation, 'fill in the gaps', free to depart from wording to uphold principles in the constitution

      iii. CJEU draws on the continental tradition

      iv. Teleological approach:

6.2. Law of the EU

    i. s.2(4) European Communities Act 1972

    ii. *R v Secretary of State for Transport, ex p Factortame (No 2)* [1991] 1 All ER 70, HL/ECJ

    iii. Approach of the CJEU, see *Van Gend en Loos* [1963]

    iv. *H P Bulmer Ltd v J Bollinger SA* [1974] Ch 401 (CA)

    v. *Buchanan and Co Ltd v Babco Forwarding and Shipping (UK) Ltd* [1977] 2 WLR 107 (CA),

    vi. The modern purpose approach is more in line with this than the traditional literal integration of the common law.

    vii. Examples:

    viii. *Garland v British Rail Engineering Ltd* [1982], HL

    ix. *Duke v GEC Reliance* [1998], HL interpreting Sexual Discrimination Act 1975 s2(4), (6);

    x. *Marleasing* [1992]

    xi. *Pickstone v Freemans plc* interpreted Equal Pay Act 1970

    xii. *Litster and Others v Forth Dry Dock & Engineering Co Ltd*

    xiii. Literal interpretation *Carole Louise Webb v EMO Air Cargo (UK) Ltd No. 2* and the Sexual Discrimination Act 1975

    xiv. Purposive approach: *Grant v South Western Trains* [1988]

7. Human Rights Act 1998

7.1. Domestic Law After HRA 1998

    i. Before HRA 1998, courts were only required consider Convention rights in interpreting legislation.

    ii. After HRA 1998, the courts are required to consider the ECHR.

        a. Rule of construction

7.2. Declarations of Incompatibility

    i. s.4(1) HRA 1998

    ii. The option does not invalidate the legislation and has no effect on cases where declaration is made

    iii. Parliament can amend or repeal the provision in question (s.10 HTA 1998)

7.3. Approach of Courts

7.4. Other methods of reading a provision as compatible with the ECHR

    i. Reading Down

    ii. Reading In

    iii. Reading Out.

7.5. Examples

   i. *R v A (Complainant's Sexual History) sub nom. R v Y (Sexual Offense: Complainant's Sexual History* [2001] 2 WLR 1546

   ii. *Ghaidan v Godlin-Mendoza* [2004]

7.6. Declarations of Incompatibility and Government Responses

   i. Parliament has no obligation to remedy the incompatibility

   ii. Examples

      a. *R v (1) Mental Health Review Tribunal, North & East London Region (2) Secretary of State for Health ex p H* (2001), Mental health Act 1983, Arts 5(1) and (4) of the ECHR. Parliament amended the Act with the Mental Health Act 1983 (Remedial) Order 2001 (SI 2001/3712),

      b. Bellinger v Bellinger [2003] UKHL 21 — Section 11(c) of the Matrimonial Causes Act 1973, Arts 8 and 12 ECHR, Parliament remedied with Gender Recognition Act 2004.

      c. *A v Secretary of State for the Home Department* [2004] UKHL 56, Crime and Security Act 2001, Art 3 ECHR, repealed in Prevention of Terrorism Act 2005.

5. Judiciary

1. Constitutional Reform Act 2005
 1.1. Before the Act
  i. the head of the judiciary
  ii. position was established 1400 year ago as the secretary to the King, eventually took over other functions, such as presiding over Parliament when the king was absent
  iii. By the 1200s, he was the most senior judge in the end next to the King
  iv. In modern times, the Chancellor as the senior judge, appointment by the current Prime Minister, with a seat in the cabinet, as well as the Speaker o the House of Lord.
  v. This meant the Chancellor had a role in all three branches of government, normally a red flag for constitutional-based governments.
 1.2. After the passing of the HRA 1998 possible conflicts of interest under Art 6 of the ECHR.
  i. *McGonnell v UK* [2000]
 1.3. Constitutional Reform Act 2005
  i. Replaced Lord Chancellor as head of judiciary with the Lord Chief Justice
  ii. Established an Independent Judicial Appointments Commission

2. Hierarchy
 2.1. Supreme Court Justices (12)
  Heads of Division (5)
  Lords and Lady Justices of Appeal (35)
  High Court judges (108)
  Circuit judges (county court and Crown Court) (654)
  Recorder (part-time circuit judges) (1196)
  District judges (county court and magistrates' courts) Deputy district judges (part-time district judges)
  (Tribunals judiciary are based on seniority to court judiciary)

3. Independence of the Judiciary
 3.1. Independence is ensured by
  i. protection against being dismissed
  ii. immunity from legal action
  iii. generous pay and employment conditions
 3.2. s.3(1) CRA 2005; s.3(5) CRA 2005:

3.3. Tenure
   i. 'security of tenure during good behavior'
   ii. Can be removed from office by both of both Houses of
      Parliament
   iii. Senior Courts Act 1981; CRA 2005.
   iv. Judges below this level may be dismissed by the Lord Chief
      Justice without approval of Parliament
   v. For part-time judges, new terms were introduced in 2000;
      non-renewal of contracts can be for a variety of reasons
3.4. Immunity
   i. Cannot be sued for actions or words done in the furtherance of
      their judicial role in good faith
   ii. This applies to all superior judges, judges of inferior courts,
      and tribunal judges
   iii. *Sirros v Moore* [1974] 3 All ER 776
3.5. Salary
   i. s.3 Commissions and Salaries of Judges Act 1760, repealed in
      1879, and then provided in a number of different statutes
   ii. Reduction of salaries has not been dealt with in England
   iii. Senior Salaries Review Board reviews salaries for England
      and Wales annually, makes recommendations to Prime
      Minister and Lord Chancellor

4. Legitimacy and Authority
4.1. Impartiality
   i. nemo judex in causa sua
   ii. must not only be free from partiality, but even from the
      appearance of it
   iii. public must feel it can trust the judiciary
   iv. recusal; See *Magill v Porter* [2001] UKHL 67
4.2. The *Pinochet* case
4.3. Recusal from the Court of Appeal
   i. *Locabail (UK) Ltd v Bayfield Properties Ltd* [1999] EWCA
      Civ 3004
   ii. Recusal from HoL after HRA 1998

5. Appointments before the Constitutional Reform Act 2005
5.1. Appointment
   i. In most common law systems, judges are chosen from legal
      practitioners
   ii. Judges in England and Wales appointed by Her Majesty on
      advice of minsters
5.2. Importance to the Public

     i. democratic deficit because they are not elected like the other branches

     ii. The public confidence from the Judiciary's professionalism and expertise

  5.3. Diversity and Legitimacy

     i. Recent concerns about the judiciary question its composition

6. Appointments Before the Constitutional Reform Act 2005

  6.1. The Process

     i. Before 1990 apppointments were limited to qualified barristers:

     ii. After 1990, the Courts and Legal Services Act (CLSA) 1990 was passed

     iii. Eligibility was further broadened under the Tribunals, Courts and Enforcement Act (TCE Act) 2007

     iv. Before the 1990s judicial appointments are made by department

       a. The organization JUSTICE report in 1992

       b. The report also argued for modern appointment procedures to increase diversity

       c. Many of these improvements were made in the 1990s

  6.2. Peach Report on Judicial Appointments 1999

     i. He concluded the process was thorough, competent, and professional and as good as any in the public sector

     ii. He recommended the establishment of a commission for judicial appointments

  6.3. Commission for Judicial Appointments 2001–2005

     i. To hear complaints about the system, audit the process (but not to appoint judges)

     ii. The commissioners identified a number of problems in the system

     iii. Recommended that the commission be dissolved an independent judicial appointments commission be established

  6.4. Judicial Appointment Process Before 2006

     i. Criticism was that the group lacked diversity that matched population

     ii. In 2004 the first female member was appointed the House of Lords (Baroness Hale of Richmond)

7. Selection Process After CRA 2005

  7.1. Argument for Change by the Government

     i. 2003— Secretary of State for constitutional affairs issued a

consultation paper
- a. To reinforce the constitutional separation of powers
- b. To increase the diversity of the judiciary

ii. The CRA 2005 establish this judicial appointments commission

iii. The Crime and Courts Act 2013:

7.2. Judicial Appointments Commission

i. Responsible for candidates to the High Court and and all courts In tribunals below

ii. Is involved in the appointments to Courts of Appeals, heads of division, and Supreme Court

iii. The commissions obligations
- a. Selections are made solely on merit
- b. Selections are only people of good character
- c. The commission should have regard for the need of diversity (the commission was not required to increase the diversity but widen the pool of candidates available)

7.3. Appointment on Merit

i. Intellectual capacity

ii. Personal qualities

iii. The ability to understand and deal fairly

iv. Exhibit authority and communication

v. Exhibit leadership and management skills

7.4. The Process

i. Includes:
- a. application forms and references
- b. Short listing and a possible test
- c. Interviews with candidates
- d. Role playing
- e. Statutory consultation
- f. Character background checks

ii. Objectives
- a. Modernize the process
- b. Broaden the pool of candidates
- c. Establish a program of education and publicity of the work of the Commission
- d. Dispel myths about judicial appointments
- e. Encourage underrepresented qualified candidates

8. Increasing Diversity

8.1. The 2004 paper 'Increasing diversity in the judiciary' by the Department for Constitutional Affairs, described the reason why

the government thought the change in the judiciary mattered:
8.2. Three topics"
- i. Equal opportunities for all qualified people on the merits without regard to gender, skin color, ethnic origin, class, sexuality, disability, etc.
- ii. The legitimacy of the judiciary is hurt by a lack of diversity because of the power that an elected group has if it's composition does not reflect society as a whole
- iii. Of varied and wider composition of the judiciary Will bring broader perspectives to the legal issues addressed
  - a. Since the decisions of the courts Will impact all areas of society at sometime, a judiciary that brings background from all those areas Will be more just

8.3. Progress
- i. The JAC strategy consisted of three elements
  - a. Make the process fair and non-discriminatory
  - b. advertising and outreach to encourage wide pool of candidates
  - c. work with other organizations to remove barriers to wide pool of candidates
- ii. Number of women appointed to judiciary has increased, other areas have not grown as expected
- iii. April 2009: the Lord Chancellor to set up an Advisory Panel on Judicial Diversity, chaired by Baroness Neuberger
  - a. The Panel suggested 53 measures to increase diversity, which were accepted by the Lord Chief Justice
- iv. May 2012: House of Lords Constitution Committee
  - a. The judicial appointment selection committee should include laypersons
  - b. The judicial appointments committee goal should be extended to the Lord Chancellor and order Chief Justice
  - c. s.159 of the Equality Act 2010 should be part of the appointment process ('tipping provision')
  - d. Within five years, if there is no significant increase in the goals, the government should consider Setting targets (Nonmandatory)
- v. Some of the suggested changes were introduced into the Crime and Courts Act 2013
- vi. Dec 2014: statistics of the judicial appointment commission show the number of women has increased, the number of black and minority ethnic lawyers what is still low and

perhaps decreasing
8.4. Crime and Courts Act 2013
  i. equal merit provision or 'tipping' provision)
  ii. This provision has been controversial
8.5. Reasons for lack of progress
  i. Experience
  ii. Self-exclusion
  iii. Bias
  iv. Merit

9. Judicial Power and Relationship to the Executive and Legislative
9.1. Shift from democracy to 'juristocracy'?
9.2. Vernon Bogdanor, leading political scientist, argued reasons for this shift (2006):
9.3. Advances in technology have led to ethical challenges are new to the world
  i. Life and death, abortion, privacy, etc.
  ii. *Re A (Children)* [2000] EWCA Civ 254

10. Protection of Human Rights
10.1. All public bodies except Parliament have the duty to function within convention rights unless excluded specifically by primary legislation (s.6 HRA 1998)
10.2. Created a shift in the balance of power and tensions between the executive, legislative, and courts
10.3. Led to increasings calls for Britain to exit the EU (referendum to be held on 23 June 2016)

11. Terrorism
11.1. Anti-Terrorism, Crime and Security Act of 2001
  i. *A and X v Secretary of State for the Home Department* [2004] UKHL 56 (the *Belmarsh* case)
  ii. ACSA repealed and passed a new Act, the Prevention of Terrorism Act 2005
11.2. Closed proceedings and the principle of openness
  i. *Al Rawi v The Security Service* [2011] UKSC 34
  ii. Justice and Security Act (JSA) 2013
11.3. Prisoner voting rights
  i. In *Hirst (No 2) v UK* (2005), *Greens v UK* (2010) and *Scoppola v Italy* (2012))
  ii. *R (on the application of Chester) v Secretary of State for Justice* [2013] UKSC 63
  iii. Voting Eligibility (Prisoners) Draft Bill in Nov 2012
11.4. Does HRA 1998 give too much power to the judiciary?

6. Civil Justice System

1. Civil v Criminal
    1.1. The purpose of civil justice is usually redress,
    1.2. Who initiates
      i. the claimant
      ii. the defendant or respondent
    1.3. Burden and standard of proof
      i. The responsibility proof
      ii. The standard of proof is on the balance of probabilities
    1.4. Most civil cases are decided by judges or magistrates, rarely by Juries
    1.5. Penalties
      i. Financial compensation
      ii. Injunction or declaration
      iii. Other

2. Scope
    2.1. The civil justice system is more broad and complex than the criminal system
      i. The range of claimants and defendants is broad
      ii. The areas of law are broad
      iii. The goals of accessibility, affordability, efficiency, fairness, injustice, can be difficult because of the complexity
      iv. Public courts set up and run by the state apply for the common law and statutes for citizens
      v. Private dispute resolution (ADR) options are also available

3. Public Good
    3.1. Introduction
      i. It has a dispute resolution options to avoid high costs of litigation
      ii. Supports social order and economic activity
      iii. To enforce governmental duties and a check on the misuse of power
      iv. Publicity of proceedings and adjudication
    3.2. Process
      i. Most disputes, especially contracts or commercial or consumer transactions, are settled by direct negotiation between parties

ii. Dispute resolution, Arbitration, and mediation are available when the third party is needed to resolve the dispute

iii. If these options do not result in a solution, or if a defendant is unwilling to address the dispute, the court has the power to compel and decide the case

iv. The court system and the process have a clear structure
   a. litigation
   b. litigants
   c. Issue of Proceedings
   d. defense
   e. One of three tracks
   f. Trial preparation
   g. Trial

3.3. Settlements

i. Can continue to negotiate even after court proceedings have begun

ii. Most cases are settled before trial (usually through the parties attorneys at this stage)

3.4. Civil Justice and Rule of Law

i. The W JP regards the following as necessary for a proper civil justice system
   a. Accessibility
   b. Affordability
   c. Effectiveness
   d. Impartiality
   e. Cultural competence

3.5. Accessibility barriers

i. Not being aware of rights

ii. Unaware of where to find advice and assistance

iii. Inability to pay for professional representation

iv. Inability to understand a complex legal system

3.6. Access to civil justice and legal aid

i. The Legal Aid and Advice Act 1949

ii. By the mid 1990s the cost of the system was about 2 billion

iii. The Legal Aid, Sentencing and Punishment of Offenders Act 2012 removed legal aid for almost all of civil and family cases

iv. November 2014 report: 'implementing the forms to civil legal aid'

v. March 2015: the House of Commons justice committee released the results of an inquiry to examine the changes in

civil legal aid
  a. The conclusions were critical of the Act because it failed to meet three of its 4 key objectives:
  b. The Act had reduced the cost of the system, but failed to meet the other three objectives
  c. Conclusions
      - The ministry was not able to ensure that all who are eligible were able to access legal aid
      - The Act lead to cutting or downsizing in the legal aid market and publicly funded services, leading to concerns about the sustainability of the entire system
      - Cases by litigants-in-person had increased substantially, which results in more time and expense to the courts and assistance to them
      - There had been a significant decrease in the use of mediation, The opposite of what had been predicted
3.7. Should there be a right to civil access?
  i. *Witham* [1998] 2 WLR 849
  ii. *R (Daly) v Secretary of State for the Home Department* [2001] 2 AC 532
  iii. The right of equal treatment is also recognized by the common law
  iv. Art 6(3) HRA 1998; not in Art 6 ECHR
      a. *Airey v Ireland* 32 Eur Ct HR Ser A (1979): [1979] 2 EHRR 305
  v. Some argue that there is a common law right to civil legal aid

4. Making Civil Justice Accessible
  4.1. Woolf Reforms (interim report 1995, final report 1996)
      i. Wolf proposed a system of proportionality
      ii. Proposed different civil tracks: simple cases when used quick and clear procedures, The more complicated cases would you use more complex procedures
      iii. Proposed the promotion of early settlement, use of the courts should be a last resort
      iv. ADR and meditation, private
  4.2. Civil Procedure Rules (1999)
      i. Designed to be easy to understand
      ii. CPR Part 1.1 'enabling the court to deal with cases justly another proportionate cost'
      iii. Judges manage the cases and encourage cooperation, identifying key issues, encourage settlement through ADR,

efficiency
iv. Three procedural tracks
    a. Small claims track (CPR Part 27)
    b. The fast track (CPR Part 28)
    c. The multi-track (CPR Part 29)
4.3. Legal Costs
    i. Since these reforms, Analysis shows that it has been partially successful in promoting cooperation, settlement, and reducing Delay
    ii. The reforms do not seem to have lowered the costs
    iii. Lord Justice Jackson was commissioned to review litigation costs
        a. The complexity of the procedure had been increased in some ways
        b. Jackson's reforms or implemented in April 2013,
4.4. Increase of Litigants In Person (LIP)
4.5. LIPs and the adversarial nature of law
    i. Research shows that LIPs having difficulty understanding the law, Collecting evidence, following procedural rules, and are at a disadvantage in arguing their cases
    ii. *Re R (A Child)* [2014] EWCA Civ 597 -
    iii. The civil justice council recommended simplification of the law, process, and case management (2011)
    iv. A judicial working group (2013) recommended a more inquisitorial approach for cases involving LIPs
4.6. Adversarial v inquisitorial
    i. Need for flexibility to adapt inquisitorial approaches in cases with LIPs
        a. *Mole v Hunter* [2014] EWHC 658 (QB)
        b. *Re C (A Child)* [2013] EWCA Civ 1412, *Re W (A Child)* [2013] EWCA Civ 1227, *Re D (A Child)* [2014] EWCA Civ 315
    ii. The national audit office, *report on implementation of legal aid reforms*, November 2014 found that LIPS:
        a. Less likely to settle
        b. Have more court orders and interventions
        c. Do not have the knowledge and skills to conduct the case efficiently
        d. Caused more work for judges and court staff, which makes the court process inefficient
    iii. Civil justice council, third for him on litigants in person,

December 2014, noted
  a. The need for a coherent strategy
  b. Organizations must collaborate on a system
  c. Paralegals and students could help be part of the solution
  d. Basic assistance is needed to litigants in person
  e. Need to simplify court procedure
  f. Need to train the judiciary

5. Alternative Dispute Resolution

5.1. Types
  i. Arbitration
  ii. Early Neutral Evaluation
  iii. Expert Determination
  iv. Mediation
  v. Conciliation
  vi. Med-Arb
  vii. Ombudsmen

5.2. The common law and mediation
  i. The voluntary use of mediation between 1996 and 2001 remain low
  ii. The courts addressed the issue in a number of cases
    a. *Cowl v Plymouth City Council* [2001] EWCA Civ 1935
    b. *Dunnett v Railtrack plc* [2002] EWCA Civ 2003
    c. *Hurst v Leeming* [2001] EWHC 1051 (Ch)
    d. *Halsey v Milton Keynes General NHS Trust* [2004] EWCA (Civ) 576
    e. *PGF II SA v OMFS Company* [2012] EWHC 83 (TCC) ance of success in mediation, the court shall consider the refusal in exercising discretion for awarding costs

5.3. Mandatory mediation
  i. The government supports a mandatory mediation System (which has been used for some civil and family cases in Australia and Canada)
  ii. Some members of the Judiciary, legal practitioners, and others are opposed (see Menkel Meadow's arguments)
  iii. CPR 26.4

5.4. Evaluating ADR
  i. Positives
    a. Can enable a dispute to end more quickly
    b. Less expensive for the parties
    c. Allows the parties to engage directly rather than through the adversarial process through their attorneys

      d. Some argue that ADR processes increase access to justice
    ii. Negatives
      a. Some research shows that Power imbalances between the parties maybe a disadvantage the the weaker party
      b. The access to justice improvement has been questioned (See Genn, 2009, [age 117)
  5.5. Online dispute resolution
    i. February 2015 report by the Civil Justice Council suggested
      a. Online dispute avoiding services
      b. Online facilitation to resolve disputes
      c. Online dispute resolution by judges

6. Trials, Privatization, Rule of Law

  6.1. Since the mid-1990s, case is going to trial have decreased dramatically ('the vanishing trial' phenomenon)
  6.2. Criticism to the loss of precedent in common-law systems, because private dispute resolution happens outside the system (see Genn (2013))
  6.3. Others believe this is simply part of a positive evolution of the Anglo-American system
  6.4. Still, it is true that an increase in prelitigation settlement, arbitration, and mediation, will have an impact in many areas of law
    i. It will lead to a loss of guidance in the law
    ii. It will lead to the loss of justice seen by the public
    iii. Does this undermine the rule of law principal that legal rules are to be known and adjudicated in public for the continuing good of the system

7. Criminal Justice System

1. Purpose
   1.1. Key purposes
      i. Prevent and deter criminal behavior
      ii. Investigation
      iii. Evidence gathering
      iv. Arresting, charging, prosecuting
      v. Punishment of those found guilty
   1.2. Key organizations
      i. The police.
      ii. Crown Prosecution Service.
      iii. Courts, judges, juries
      iv. Criminal Cases Review Commission
   1.3. ECHR articles with influence
      i. Right to a fair trial (Art 6)
      ii. Freedom from arbitrary detention (Art 5)
      iii. Freedom from inhumane and degrading treatment (Art 3)
      iv. Right to privacy (Art 8)

2. Police and Police Powers
   2.1. Police and Criminal Evidence Act 1984
   2.2. Codes of Practice (s.66)
   2.3. Stop and Search; s.1 PACE police Power to stop and search people in public
   2.4. Arrest and Detention
      i. *Spicer v Holt* (1977); *R v Lemsatef* [1977]
      ii. s.24 PACE was amended by Serious Organised Crime and Police Act 2005

3. Crown Prosecution Service
   3.1. Prosecution of Offenses Act 1985
   3.2. Prosecutorial Discretion, CPS Code
   3.3. Public Interest (e.g., Assisted Suicide as example)
      i. s.2(1), 2(4) Suicide Act 1961; *R (Purdy) v DPP* [2009] UKHL 45
      ii. *R (on the application of Nicklinson) v Ministry of Justice* [2014] UKSC 38
   3.4. Evaluating the CPS
      i. Lord Justice Glidewell Report; Government White Paper,

'justice for all' (2002); Criminal Justice Act 2003
4. Courts, Judges, Juries
    4.1. Classification of Crimes
      i. Summary Offenses
      ii. Triable-Either-Way Offenses
      iii. Indictable Offenses
    4.2. Trial and Case Management
      i. 'Justice for All' White Paper
      ii. Criminal Just Act 2003
      iii. The 2005 Criminal Procedure Rules sought to improve
        efficiency of trials
    4.3. Magistrate Courts
    4.4. Crown Courts
5. Juries
    5.1. Juries Use in the Courts
      i. Criminal Trials
      ii. Civil Trials
      iii. Coroners' Courts
    5.2. Function and Independence
      i. To decide matters of fact
      ii. The decision is final (*Bushell's Case* (1670) Vaughn 135)
    5.3. Unanimous verdicts were required until 1967; majority allowed
      after
    5.4. Qualifications
      i. Before 1972 a juror had to be a property owner, after Juries
        Act 1974 did not
      ii. A judge may remove a person from jury service if they
        believe the lack capacity (lack of English skills, a disability)
    5.5. Selection
      i. Selected at random by the Jury Central Summoning Bureau
        from the electoral register
      ii. A court official chooses from the pool two here particular
        cases
    5.6. Excusal
      i. Criminal Justice Act 2003
      ii. Bias and professionals sitting on juries
        a. *R v Abdroikof, R v Green and R v Williamson* [2007]
          UKHL 37, [2007] 1 WLR 2679
        b. *Hanif v UK* (2012)
6. Independence and Impartiality
    6.1. s.8(1) Contempt of Court Act 1981; *Taxquet v Belgium* (2012)

54 EHRR 26

6.2. *R v Mirza* [2004] UKHL 2

6.3. *AG v Scotcher* [2005] UKHL 36, [2005] 1 WLR 1867

6.4. Race and Fairness

   i. *R v Ford* [1989] 3 All ER 445 — judges are not obligated to create multi racial juries

   ii. Runciman Commission 1993

   iii. Government White Paper 2002 ('Justice for All') — opposed the selection of multi racial juries

   iv. *R v Smith* [2003] EWCA Crim 283

   v. *Sander v UK* [2000] ECHR 194

6.5. Fairness and the Internet

   i. Contempt of Court

      a. Art 6 ECHR

      b. *AG v Dallas* [2012] EWHC 156 (Admin); *AG v Davey*; *AG v Beard* [2013] EWHC 2317 (Admin), [2013] All ER (D) 391

   ii. Strengthening the laws

      a. Criminal Justice and Courts Act 2015

         - s.71 — offense for a juror to intentionally research information during the trial period, where he knows or reasonably knows that the information maybe or is relevant to the case

         - s.72 — offense for one juror to pass to another juror information found by research not presented in court

         - s.73 — offense for unsure in a case before a court to purposefully engage in prohibited conduct during the trial.

         - s.74 — offense to intentionally disclose information about jury deliberations, or to solicit such information

6.6. Non-jury trials

   i. s. 44 Criminal Justice Act 2003

   ii. *J, S, M v R* [2010] EWCA Crim 1755; *KS v R* [2010] EWCA Crim 1756

7. Appeals

7.1. Prosecution appeals

   i. s.36 Criminal Justice Act 1972 point of law

   ii. s.36 Criminal Justice Act 1988 sentence too lenient;

   iii. s.75–76 Criminal Justice Act 2003 new and compelling evidence/public interest

7.2. Defense appeals

i. magistrates Court to Crown Court

ii. Crown Court to Court of Appeal (criminal division)
  a. Criminal Appeal Act 1968

iii. Supreme Court,

7.3. Criminal Cases Review Commission

i. Royal Commission on Criminal Justice Report (1993)

ii. Criminal Appeal Act 1995 — established the Criminal Cases Review Commission

iii. The Innocence Network UK report (Feb 2013)

iv. House of Commons Justice Committee Report (Mar 2015)

ABOUT THE AUTHORS

Dr. Markus McDowell holds a law degree from the University of London. He is the Editor-in-Chief of the *Legal Issues Journal* and writes articles for Legal Yankee, a website of resources for law students in the UK and the US.

Jessica Patel is a freelance paralegal, graphic designer, and writer. She is a staff writer and researcher for Legal Yankee, a website of resources for law students in the UK and the US.

Made in the USA
Lexington, KY
10 April 2016